When Heads and Hearts Collide

My Personal Journey in Parenting My Parents

Arline Chandler

FLYING HORSE PRESS

Cover design: Linda Warwick

Library of Congress Catalog Card Number: 98-93284

ISBN: 0-9657975-1-1

10 9 8 7 6 5 4 3 2 1

Ordering information:

When Heads and Hearts Collide is available for purchase by check or money order for $12.00 plus $2.50 shipping and handling from:

Flying Horse Press
210 South Ninth Street
Heber Springs, Arkansas 72543

Booking information:

For booking information on Mrs. Chandler's seminars on *The Nursing Home Decision and Caring for Aging Parents*, call

(501) 362-3420 or e-mail: chandler@arkansas.net.

To my parents,
Arlie and Loree Ramsey,
who are now at peace in their Heavenly Home.

CONTENTS

INTRODUCTION

Statistics support the fact that people are living longer and more productive lives. While the extended time to enjoy our parents' wisdom and companionship is cause for rejoicing, almost every family eventually comes to grips with that dreaded question: What happens when Mother and Dad can no longer take care of themselves?

My parents' declining health and their ability to make sound decisions about their personal matters came about gradually. But one morning following a battle of wills—Mother's and mine—she screamed at me: "I want to be my own boss!"

Words I'd once yelled at her in my teenage years. And the harsh reality of a role reversal that neither of us wanted slapped me in the face. My thoughts raced over the expectations my husband and I had for some "free time" between child-rearing and our own senior years. I wanted to scream back at Mother: "I don't want to be your boss. . . ."

However, her child-like face staring back from a reclining position in the dark leather chair she occupied most of her waking hours held my tongue in check. There were daily needs that Mother and Dad could no longer meet for themselves. Instead of being the parents, they needed parenting. The circumstances left me no choice in responsibilities. Regardless of what each of us wanted, I had entered one of life's most challenging phases: Parenthood Part II.

As the months of caring and coping with my aging parents blurred into years, I found no pat answers. But I did discover that God wastes no experience in our lives. Any skills I'd acquired in raising three children and teaching scores of five-year-olds in a classroom setting were once again put to use in maintaining my parents' well-being. However, bending to tie their shoes, addressing envelopes, and color-coding medications were easy tasks compared to the heart-wrenching decisions concerning their long-term care. When a nursing home loomed as our final option, I found that the emotional skirmishes between parent and child were only beginning.

I had never expected to take responsibility for my parents' affairs. No more than they had ever expected living in their own home would end. Even after several years of walking through the door of the nursing center, the thought of my parents living in an alien place churned my emotions. Their tiny room, at first shared together, then with different roommates, was not home. It would never be. Yet, I'm thankful that my mother and dad could live in a clean, supportive institution where they were loved and cared for properly.

In the case of my family, the decision to enter my parents in a long-term nursing facility was the best choice for covering their physical, financial, and medical needs. But "right" for one family may be unacceptable for another. When the time comes for alternate living arrangements, each family must make this personal decision according to their unique situation.

The frustrations, the tears, and the tough decisions I wrestled over many sleepless nights are mixed with love, joy, and even laughter on the following pages. My hope is to help others understand how I hurt for my parents—and for myself and my family—as we traveled together down the hardest road of our lives. I longed to impart hope and peace of mind to Mother and Dad, but the day came when I had to say, "I've done everything I can to make you physically comfortable, but I cannot make you happy. Only you, drawing from your faith in God, can change your mindset."

I don't know why their last years had to be lived out in the confines of a nursing center. But I do know God plans for every stage of our lives. He promises in Jeremiah 29:11 (TLB): "For I know the plans I have for you, plans for good and not for evil, to give you a future and a hope."

"A future and a hope—in a nursing home?" Mother and Dad both asked. "You don't live here; you don't understand."

Indeed, I did not. "But someday, I may," I told them. "And I pray that when it's my turn to fill a space in a nursing home that I can hold onto whatever future God plans for me."

I could not change my parents' attitude. I could only adjust my own and set my sights on

. . . His mighty power at work within us (that) is able to do far more than we would ever dare to ask or even dream of . . . infinitely beyond our highest prayers, desires, thoughts, or hopes.

EPHESIANS 4:20 (TLB)

Chapter One

A PARENTING ROLE WITH DIFFERENT RULES

During my years as a kindergarten teacher, a procession of five-year-olds came through my classroom door with tear-filled eyes and arms locked tightly around their mothers' legs. Their fears on that first day of school tugged at my heart.

One child, I learned later, thought he would always sleep overnight at school. Another frail, tow-headed boy played all that first day with an old phone on the shelf. Over and over his fingers turned the rotary dial. When his mother appeared in the afternoon, he rushed into her arms sobbing, "I called you all day. Why didn't you answer?"

Then the roles reversed. I held my mother's arm, guiding her into a new phase of life—a nursing center. Her eyes filled with tears; her hands clung to me; her voice begged to go home. She rebelled against rules. Angry words spouted from her lips.

Like the youngsters I nurtured through a school year, she braved new experiences and encountered different people. And like the parents who entrusted me with their little ones, I had no choice but to rely on those professionally trained to care for my mother.

A GRADUAL SWITCH

Actually, the clues that our parent-child roles were reversing began long before I resigned my kindergarten teaching position. I remember one September afternoon, the thermometer sizzled at 100 degrees, prompting school officials to dismiss classes early. As I hurried down the steamy street carrying tote bags of lesson plans, my mind focused on stepping into my cool living room. A carpenter remodeling my neighbor's house stood in her doorway holding out a phone receiver.

"Telephone," he called out.

"For me? Here?" I questioned.

Stepping over saw horses, nails, and planks, I answered with a hesitant, "Hello?"

"Where have you been?" Mother's voice fumed on the other end.

"I've been at school. It's Monday," I retorted.

While she continued to fret as though I'd stayed out past a midnight curfew, I watched the workmen with quieted saws and hammers stand on one foot, then the other, waiting for me to end the conversation so they could get back on the job.

A BACKWARD LOOK

Now, looking back over the years when I gradually became my mother's mother, the frustration of her not understanding my personal responsibilities—of believing that a mother's role is to know a child's whereabouts at all times, despite the child's age approaching the mid-century mark—pales compared to the weightier matter of Mother and Dad facing the problems of illnesses and aging that eventually led to a nursing home.

When I ended my teaching career, packed up my school books, and set up an office at home for freelance writing, I envisioned quiet afternoons alone with the aroma of supper bubbling on the stove. I imagined creating characters and story plots in my cozy nook.

Mother puffed in pride at any recognition I received, but the actual work of writing she perceived much like jotting down a grocery list on the way to the store. Because I didn't go to school each morning, in her words I, ". . . no longer had to work."

Her comprehension of my lifestyle, coupled with the fact that I had set up housekeeping only two blocks away while my sister made her home on the Texas Gulf Coast, made it quite natural for both mother and Dad to depend on me for help with their daily lives. And my life-long pattern of feeling responsible for the world propelled me into action. After all, Mother and Dad had cared for me. I felt duty-bound to make their lives as comfortable and entertaining as possible.

A ONE-WOMAN SHOW

As I down-shifted from a demanding teaching schedule to an at-home writer, their distress calls came more frequently. Instead of spending hours at my typewriter with story ideas pulsing from my brain to my fingers, my life closely resembled a one-woman tennis match. Every day I raced between our houses, keeping up with their doctors' appointments and shopping.

Figuring out which one of Mother's illnesses actually needed medical attention and which ones she thought were life-threatening conditions kept me running. Noting her symptoms of ill health subsided whenever we had "fun," I planned short trips, picnics, and birthday lunches at the city mall.

While the details of running two houses clamored for my attention, I stubbornly clung to my link with the outside world in snatches of words I put together in odd moments. But one afternoon, I faced the state of my writing career when I sat down at my desk—not to type a story—but to draw bold numerals on a calendar so Mother and Dad could read the correct date.

Alone in my home office, I laughed aloud. Possibly at that very moment, my colleagues, wrestling with problems in the classroom, pictured me lounging in front of the afternoon soaps. Yet, I was repeating the same tasks I had done for years.

As I finished the calendar and tackled a stack of research clippings waiting to be filed under subjects for future articles, my phone rang.

"What's Tim's phone number?" Mother asked. "I think he'd like a call from his grandmother."

Slowly, I recited the digits.

She interrupted, "Is that 2-3-3-8?"

"No," I said.

She sounded frustrated. I paused and took a deep breath. "Let's begin again."

After going over the number again, which she repeated while Dad wrote on a notepad, I hung up. Three minutes later, another call interrupted my work. She had failed to get the numbers in sequence. I reiterated the same conversation through five phone calls.

This is the same mother who boasted last week in the doctor's waiting room, "My daughter writes all the time!"

I pushed aside my filing, wrote the number on a card, and took it over to their house. Tomorrow will be better, I said to myself.

MORE OF THE SAME

But the next day—and weeks—were no different. Mother often fell, fortunately without breaking any bones. Although I took her in for the doctor to check out her sore joints and aching muscles, she always insisted for several weeks that bones were broken. Once she contended that her shoulder was cracked. The doctor ordered X rays to give her—and himself—peace of mind.

I began to see a pattern in Mother's keeping on and on about something she wanted. If she could not get my attention, she would turn to Daddy, knowing how difficult it was for me to refuse him.

And I figured out Dad's philosophy. It was easier to give in than to argue. On one hand, he knew that Mother's ailments were not as serious as she imagined. But on the other hand, he defended every pain, relating to family and friends, "She's not doing well. I've never seen anyone suffer like she did last night. . . ." Or yesterday—or whenever Mother told him she hurt.

DAD TO THE RESCUE

And while her life revolved around one ache after another, Dad took over the household cleaning, cooking, shopping, and laundry. Mother thought nothing of asking his stiff-jointed, out-of-breath body to fetch her glasses of juice or redo the housework that did not meet her standard of perfection.

One day, following an examination Mother had deemed absolutely necessary, our family physician called me aside and confided: "Your mother has the aches and pains typical of women her age, but I can't find anything significantly wrong. She is manipulating you with her complaints."

"But for most of my life, I've believed that when she hurt, it was worse than anyone else," I told him. "I can't judge whether the pain is real or mild—or imagined."

A TURNING POINT

But I began to understand the doctor's viewpoint when Mother phoned one afternoon describing a rash. "I have red whelps all over my back and legs and even red bumps under my skin," she related, "My mouth—and my stomach—are broken out."

Remembering that once she did indeed have a reaction to medication that turned her entire body into angry, reddish-purple splotches, I left house guests and hurried to check her out. But I couldn't find one bump. I beamed Dad's magnified reading lamp over her arms and legs. There was no rash. But she insisted, "You just can't see it!"

"Mother, when you tell me you have a headache or a backache, I can't see that," I told her. "But I can see a rash, and it's just not there."

I could not dissuade her, so I finally returned home, thinking over some other tactics I might try to take Mother's mind off herself. *Maybe I'm helping her too much*, I thought.

BACKING OFF

A few days later, I drove both my parents home from a doctor's appointment. Instead of warning Mother to sit still until I jumped out, ran around to the passenger side and opened the door, I stayed in the driver's seat while she unbuckled her seat belt. She opened her door and slipped to the curb, teetering back and forth until she balanced between the seat and the door. Watching her shaky attempt to get out of a vehicle, I felt like a mother abandoning her child.

His movements equally uncoordinated, Dad climbed out the back door. He trailed behind Mother like a puppy with its nose to the ground. Their frailty brought tears to my eyes. One moment, their halting steps pounded on my heart; the next, I determined to push them toward greater independence.

Holding to the porch handrail, Mother pulled herself up the three steps. Dad followed on her heels. When she reached the top, I saw her lose her balance and fall backwards, bumping Dad and pushing him off the second step and smack into the middle of a shrub by the sidewalk.

My heart pounding in my throat, I jumped out of my van, picked them up and brushed them off. Checking the two over for bruises and broken bones, I mentally kicked myself. Despite the doctor's diagnosis that Mother had no major problems, something was wrong—something that prompted her falls and lack of coordination.

Be not anxious about anything, but in everything, by prayer and petition, with thanksgiving, present your requests to God. And the peace of God, which transcends all understanding, will guard your hearts and your minds in Christ Jesus.

PHILIPPIANS. 4:6-7 (NIV)

CHAPTER TWO

THE PROBLEM DEFINED

When the weakness in Mother's legs, along with her headaches, persisted, making her stumble more often, the doctor ordered a series of tests. We often left home at dawn to drive to a nearby city for the appointments. After a succession of doctors came to no firm conclusion, she was referred to a neurologist. He took one look at her shuffling steps crossing his office threshold and said: "Parkinson's."

When she heard his words, I will never forget the despair on Mother's face, the slump of her body in utter helplessness. My own senses fought desperation, wanting to wrap her in my arms and hold back the ravages of old age. More than anything in the world, I wanted to share with her my own vitality, my passion for meeting people, for seeing the world. Beating against the invisible wall of her defeated spirit brought to mind a game of fourth-grade baseball when a bat slammed into my stomach, leaving me on the ground gasping for breath.

While my emotions played tug-of-war, the doctor dismissed her condition as slight. "I don't believe it will progress to a debilitating stage," his words continued. He prescribed no medication since he found no evidence of any other neurological problems.

My ears heard his words, but my eyes were fixed on Mother's vulnerable face. I knew her well. Parkinson's, although at that moment an unknown condition to me, would only add to the list of ailments Mother obsessed on and refused to fight with any reasoning.

SEEKING SOLUTIONS

I turned and tossed that night, repeating the question that had become a standard opener for all my conversations: *What am I going to do with Mother and Dad?* Although the next morning's drab light came through my window punctuated by cold January raindrops, a name whispered through my muddled thoughts like a fresh spring breeze. My friend from painting class. A physical therapist. She could help. Surely, I believed, God had brought her to mind.

Her voice on the other end of the phone assured me that physical therapy would help with Mother's symptoms. She told me the procedure to follow to get a doctor's order.

Our family doctor, more skeptical about its benefit, reluctantly ordered the therapy for Mother's condition. However, unlike the neurologist, he prescribed medication for Parkinson's.

Armed with two kinds of pills and the therapist's encouragement, we began a new schedule. Three days every week we visited her office. Then we practiced the same routine of dance steps and leg-lifts each morning at home.

How awkward Mother and I looked in the beginning, our arms locked like polka partners, stepping sideways and backward across the kitchen floor. But her balance improved slightly and her stamina increased. In a month, she had worked up to lifting a ten-pound weight on each leg.

When the therapist showed us how she could sit in a chair behind a stationary bicycle and pedal for thirty-minute intervals, we moved my bike to her house. The daily schedule tightened. Although Mother told everyone she worked hard, she forgot the mornings I pushed, prodded, and pulled her into action. When we went into the therapist's office, she recounted how good she had felt the day before.

FRUSTRATION BOILED OVER

"I wish you'd told me, Mother. I don't remember your feeling good," I commented, although she ignored my agitation.

When the therapist told her to do housework to keep herself in shape, Mother continued, "Oh, I do all my work. . . ." And she recapped the chores that Dad did. I stood behind her shaking my head.

Although I tried to mask my feelings with a cheery "good morning," I dreaded opening my parents' front door—the door of a house that once had been my haven from the world. At that point, their home had taken on Mother's depressed state.

KEEPING IT LIGHT

I tried to brighten the mood with a Garfield® poster captioned: "I might as well exercise; I'm already in a bad mood!"

Mother taped it to her refrigerator, but the humor was lost. She believed that cures for pain, disease, even fatigue, came in pills, doctor's examinations, or hospital stays. In her mind, nothing as simple as exercise could alter a physical condition.

I remember the day she retorted, "When I'm dead, you'll pass by my casket and say, 'Get up and walk, Mother. You'll feel better!'"

TWO EXTREMES

While I cajoled her into action, Dad presented a different set of problems. Mother wanted to do nothing. Dad tried to do everything. Like a drowning man grasping a rope, he held onto his last shreds of independence—driving his car, taking care of Mother, cooking, and cleaning. A tall order for a man with severely limited eyesight, poor hearing, a pacemaker, and a body that could no longer keep up with his quick mind.

"I can see things in the distance," he would tell me. But when he asked for help distinguishing a bowl of lemon from a bowl of sliced onions on the dinner table, I knew he could not see a pedestrian or a child on a skateboard crossing in front of his car.

THE BLACKENED CARROTS

One day when Mother and I returned from a therapy session, I opened the door to a smoke-filled kitchen. Dad stood at the sink with a scorched pan under the cold-water spout. "The carrots boiled dry, but I caught them in time," he said.

Waving away the smoke, I peered into the pan at charred discs crusted on the bottom. "Dad, these carrots are inedible," I told him. "Let me fix you some more in the microwave."

He moved aside. But knowing that he could not discern how much water he poured in a cooking pot added to the other worries about my parents trying to manage their home. I happened in that day to "fix" things, but I could not be there around-the-clock.

SOMEONE TO SWEEP

Mother agreed with my suggestion for hiring a housekeeper because a tidy, well-appointed home came high in her priorities. But Dad was adamant that he could cook and clean. The issue became his personal stand as a productive man.

While I watched Dad's body wear out, Mother still saw the young husband who always made her decisions and stood in her stead when the going got rough. I began to feel that my parents had created a monster and handed it to me. Resentment and guilt warred with love and compassion—straining my emotions.

After months of exasperation, I overrode Dad's veto on outside help. I made arrangements for a daily delivery from "Meals on Wheels." And against further protests, I hired a housekeeper for one day a week. Dad's main concern was that no one could clean their house to suit Mother. I countered his argument by making out the weekly list of chores and supervising her work.

OVER ONE HILL TO THE NEXT HURDLE

Although the physical therapy and medication strengthened Mother's arms and legs, her coordination regressed daily. Simple acts such as bathing became unsafe for the two of them to attempt alone. Even with the sturdy grip bar my husband installed along the wall, getting Mother in and out of the tub was more than Dad could handle. I took over, seating her in warm, soapy water, then leaving her to soak while I read aloud the daily newspaper to Dad.

After a few months, their needs outnumbered my available hours, and I sought help from our local home health agencies. Following a lengthy evaluation, the county office sent an aide three mornings each week to assist Mother with personal care and exercises. Dad did not argue as long as the help came for Mother. If she had any time left over, he permitted her to read the newspaper aloud. But he made a point of taking his shower before she arrived.

LOST INDEPENDENCE

Day by day, Mother and Dad lost control of their lives. I watched it happen. But like trying to hold a tractor-trailer rig with a twine string as it balanced on a muddy embankment, I was powerless to stop it.

Dad grasped some of the situation, but his main concern was that Mother's needs—real or imagined—be met. He outlined how he wanted me to take care of Mother in the event that he died first. He stipulated that I maintain her house, even if she had to live in a nearby assisted-living facility.

Never did Dad or Mother consider the services of a nursing home, not even when the family doctor said they could no longer live alone. Dad refuted the doctor's advice to hire live-in help by pushing himself harder. And Mother believed Dad would always be there to take care of her.

FROM WHEELS TO FEET

When I convinced them to give their car to my teenage nephew, I drew a sigh of relief. At least, I would not worry about Dad killing someone on the streets. But against Mother's objections, he began walking the few blocks to town. I applauded his grit, but his unsteady legs, plus his poor eyesight and weakened heart, only replaced one worry for another. The fact that the service station attendant on the corner saw him fall one day in the middle of the town's busiest street added to my concern.

I remember the hot August day when he walked to the drug store. Mother phoned to say he had been gone for over an hour. Immediately, I set out looking for him. Knowing his heart condition could not take our Arkansas humidity, I traced his steps to the store. The clerk told me he had just left.

After circling the block, peering into store windows for a glimpse of his stooped shoulders and the fringe of white hair peeking out from under his favorite old yellow cap, I recalled how he enjoyed visiting with the hardware store owner.

Squeezing into a parking slot, I went inside the store. Dad was in the back, suspended in time with the kind of spirited conversations he had sorely missed following his retirement from the business community. I felt like a truant officer picking up a hooky-playing child.

"Dad, I've come to drive you home. It's too hot for you to walk this morning," I said. As I buckled him in the front seat of my van, I fussed about him crossing the major highway between his house and Main Street. "You can't see the cars coming, Dad. What if you stumbled and fell? A driver couldn't stop before hitting you."

With his usual good nature, he changed the subject. But I overheard him later explaining that he could not go to town because I wouldn't let him cross the streets.

When I took him inside his house, Mother stood on a kitchen stool, her arms and legs trembling as she reached for a coffee can on the top shelf. "I can't wait on someone to get everything," she huffed when I scolded her. Again, the question raced through my head: *What am I going to do to keep them safe?*

Trying to outguess my parents' needs, I felt like a jack-in-the-box stuffed into a metal square and trapped inside by a lid. Mother or Dad turned the handle and I jumped out in all directions.

SHELVING PERSONAL PLANS

When a woman's newspaper in Missouri offered me an assignment to interview a well-known novelist, I hoped against hope that Mother would stay well enough for me to be away overnight. But while helping with her morning bath, I spotted a rash that looked like shingles. I made a doctor's appointment, thinking I could leave an hour later and still make the interview. But my plans were dashed when he confirmed my diagnosis and prescribed a strong medication. Instinctively, I knew Mother could not keep up with the complicated dosage and Dad was too blind to help her.

She did not realize that an important opportunity passed me by. Somehow when we switched roles between parent and child, Mother lost any understanding of me as a woman living in the outside world. Because she never wanted a life beyond her own household, in old age, she focused totally on herself.

I remember when Mother's thoughts were not so self-centered. She and Dad were my first link with a heavenly Father. As a youngster, I looked to them as though they were God. Through the teenage years and into my role as wife and mother, their influence had a mysterious lifeline to His authority.

Suddenly, I was faced with reprimanding them, caring for their personal needs, and telling them what they could and could not do. It was disconcerting, especially to look through the cracks of what I once thought was perfection and see them struggling for survival.

During those last ten years, Mother and Dad strained to stay afloat in a lifestyle their aging bodies could no longer accommodate. I ached for their passing youth and independence.

In those conflicting circumstances, I am thankful that I could be there for my parents at that stage of their lives. Yet, I resented their needs dominating every waking hour. My heart was heavy because life held no challenge for them. But at the same time, I wrestled with my own mortality, seeing in them what the coming years could hold for me.

What could I do for Mother and Dad? It was the toughest question of my life. And the answers came from God's word.

I will instruct you (says the Lord) and guide you along the best pathway for your life. I will advise you and watch your progress.

PSALM 32:8 (TLB)

CHAPTER THREE

A DREADED CALL

The phone's abrupt ring startled me awake. As my husband fumbled for the receiver, I recognized Dad's strained voice coming through the line. "I need help," I heard him say, his breath gasping between the words.

We pulled on clothes and raced two blocks to my parent's home. Dad let us in and pointed to the bathroom floor where Mother lay unconscious, her eyes a glassy stare. While James worked with her, I dialed the ambulance. Dad paced between us repeating over and over, "She didn't fall; I caught her and 'easy-like' laid her on the floor." Stressing the "easy" part, he went through his actions as though he needed to prove that a fall did not cause her comatose state.

When I questioned why they were not in bed at that midnight hour, he said Mother had been seeing people in their house since the early evening newscast. He had tried to cope rather than call us.

By the time the ambulance arrived, other members of the family joined us. I insisted that Dad stay with them, assuring him there was nothing he could do at the hospital. He was upset but simply too tired to argue.

ROUND THE CLOCK VISIONS

Her hallucinations returned after Mother was admitted to a private room. Into the early morning hours, she fought snakes on the wall and people sitting beside her in bed. At one point, she insisted that the nurses had put her in a broom closet. If the situation had not been so frightening, I might have laughed. Even in her deluded state, Mother worried about a messy room!

The next morning, a breakfast tray arrived, but she believed I had taken her to a luncheon. And she let me know how embarrassed she felt at a social function wearing a hospital gown. I could not distract her even with the food on her plate.

The luncheon gave way to her claim that the sheets were soiled. Despite the fact that two nurses had to lift her from the bed to a portable commode, she gathered the linens in her arms and attempted to walk to the washing machine, thinking she was in her home. To appease her, I changed the blanket, while she still insisted that all the sheets were dirty.

A DAY LOST IN SLEEP

Nothing in my past experience had prepared me for the situation. Months before I had walked into my parents' house at mid-morning and discovered Dad dozing in his big chair while Mother curled in a fetal position in her bed. When I tried to rouse her, she gave no response. I questioned Dad, but he said he'd been waiting for me to awaken her. I decided he had fallen asleep himself and did not realize how late Mother had slept.

Nevertheless, the ambulance shrieked to their doorstep and rushed her to the hospital. For twenty-four hours, she slept as though she was drugged. The doctors explained that she had suffered a mini-stroke, more commonly called a TIA (transient ischemic attack). They could not predict the outcome. A TIA may progress to a major stroke or simply pass, they said.

Thank goodness, Mother's passed. The next morning, she opened her eyes and called her doctor's name. With no visible side effects, she returned home.

A DIFFERENT EPISODE

But this time, even the doctor was baffled. He suggested transferring her to another hospital thirty miles away where a complete neurological workup was available. I agreed and rushed home to tell Daddy. His eyes brimmed with tears as he said, "Take care of her."

But Mother fought the move, saying she had to go home first and pack a bag. However, the ambulance arrived and attendants took charge. No sedation was ordered because of the uncertainty of her condition. I feared she would struggle against the restraints they buckled across her arms and legs as they wheeled her toward the transfer vehicle. Mother's younger sister and I followed in my van.

The nurses in the new hospital shook their heads as they watched her pleat the blanket binding from one edge to the other. "Bless her heart, she'll work herself to death. They always do," they said.

"Then you've seen patients like my mother before?" I asked.

"Oh, yes," they answered, circling her bed and smoothing the covers.

But I didn't believe them. I knew something horrible had exploded inside Mother's head and she would never return to the real world.

At times her body shook so hard we would hold her arms and legs in the bed. And her delirium continued. She wanted socks on her feet. We put them on. She wanted them off. We took them off.

With grand gestures, her sister pretended to do everything she asked. We alternated ignoring and reasoning with her. But nothing reached beyond her sick fancies.

THE NIGHT'S DARKEST HOURS

Alone with Mother that night, her mind worked overtime in unreasonable confusion. She imagined Daddy had left her for another woman. My staunch and faithful Dad. Her husband for over fifty years. Again, if I had not been so scared, I would have laughed.

Looking toward the wall as though it opened onto a broad scene, she said, "Look, there he goes. . . ." With a strong, clear voice, she called his name. Then she reverted to a younger stage of life and talked about how she would manage alone with babies. At one point, she mixed up children and grandchildren, calling herself by my sister's name and identifying grandchildren as if they were her own.

When nothing calmed her, I considered phoning Dad, hoping the sound of his voice would snap Mother back to reality. But he was at home alone. I feared her state of mind would upset him.

AN OVERLOADED SYSTEM

The neurologist called in to examine Mother found no sign of stroke, brain dysfunction, or tumors in the tests he ordered. He insisted that medications had overloaded her system with toxins. I did not believe him either.

When he withdrew all her medicine, even the ones prescribed for Parkinson's, I struggled with his decision. Only a few months prior, she had shown improvement under that medication. How could it have caused this irrational state of mind and loss of motor control?

The doctor explained that sometimes Parkinson's medications build up and interact with other medicines. Although I had daily placed Mother's pills in bottles marked for breakfast, lunch, supper, and bedtime, I knew from the mixed-up containers and the pills I sometimes found on the floor that she did not take medications correctly.

I also recalled the strong round of medicine she had recently finished for a bout with shingles and the capsules prescribed for pain because she insisted her shoulder was broken following a fall. And Mother added numerous over-the-counter creams, pills, suppositories, and sprays to her prescription medicine. I had no choice but to wait out the doctor's decision.

By the time my sister arrived from her Texas home to help with round-the-clock care of Mother, the wildest hallucinations had passed. But she had returned from yet another test with no voice to her words.

Diane and I both believed the sedation given for the test triggered this new condition.

The doctor conferred with other specialists, including a speech pathologist. They found no physical evidence for her loss of voice. He expressed confidence that once her body cleared out the toxic medications, she would talk. No one on the hospital staff seemed to understand our concern that she was completely incapacitated.

A DAUGHTER KNOWS HER MOTHER—OR DOES SHE?

A few mornings later, I had my first inkling that perhaps Mother was not helpless. When I walked into her room, I found her sitting on a bedside commode with the lid closed. She indicated through hand signs and frustrated eyes that she had been there for some time and no one would help her. I summoned a nurse.

"Why is my mother sitting on this chair with the lid closed?" I asked.

"Maybe she became impatient, stood up, closed it, and sat back down," the nurse answered as she went about the task of cleaning up my mother.

"That couldn't have happened," I argued. "Mother can't physically stand up!"

"I've seen patients do lots of things I thought were impossible," she replied matter-of-factly while settling Mother into bed and hurrying out the door.

I fumed. I did not believe she could stand, no more than I believed the doctor's projection that she would walk and talk again. This was my mother in trouble. I had spent half a lifetime believing everything she said or did. How could I suddenly think she had a strength in her limbs that I could not see in her eyes?

That her condition could be . . . psychological . . . something the doctor had tactfully hinted. The doctors and nurses might be professionally trained, but I knew my mother—or so I thought.

BEGINNING THE LONG HAUL

In the meantime, the doctor told my sister and me to make arrangements for long-term care. He indicated that Mother would not be well enough to return home.

We both had known that it was only a matter of time until Mother and Dad could no longer manage in their house, even with me, the housekeeper, the yard man, home health care, and "Meals On Wheels." To give us some extra time, the staff moved Mother to a hospital wing designated for rehabilitation. They reinstated her physical therapy, setting up a schedule for bicycle pedaling and walks in the corridor. Still she could not feed herself, lift a washcloth to her face, or utter a sound.

THE ROLE REVERSAL RECOGNIZED

Diane and I traded off days and nights, making the thirty-mile commute to the hospital. One morning when I walked toward Mother's room, two therapists literally held her up, guiding her steps in a simulated walk up and down the carpeted hallway. Watching her struggle, my heart trailed behind her shuffling feet. As I matched her pace, her face stared ahead with a mask-like expression.

"I'm Mrs. Ramsey's mother," I introduced myself to the therapists.

For a moment, they held Mother steady and regarded me from head to toe. "You've held up very well, " one of them replied.

I returned their stare with equal curiosity. Our words hung between us for several seconds before I caught my slip of the tongue. I laughed with them, but the truth jabbed my consciousness. I had become my mother's mother—a role I would fill for the rest of her life on this earth.

MORE CHANGES

When Mother had been transferred to the new wing, the hospital's social services coordinator indicated that Medicare would pay up to twenty days. After two days, the staff advised me to make other arrangements immediately. Mother no longer fit their guidelines, despite the fact that her physical condition remained unchanged.

The news came at the beginning of the third week that Diane had been away from her job and family in Texas. My husband had not seen me for a meal in the same length of time. But our physical weariness did not compare to our emotional tension as we checked out the local nursing homes. We both knew Mother's contentment was enhanced in attractive surroundings, so we chose the newest and cheeriest one. But no matter how appealing, we also knew that she would not accept a new lifestyle graciously.

WHAT ABOUT DAD?

For the length of Mother's hospitalization, Diane had stayed with Dad, getting a close-up view of his failing ability to care for himself. One day when he dressed for a visit to the hospital, she noticed his new blue shirt looked like a tie-dyed version of one her sons might wear. She quickly figured out that Daddy had poured bleach directly onto the laundry before the wash cycle. Because his dimming eyes could not see the white splotches, he argued that the shirt was clean and appropriate for him to wear.

We respected his wishes to remain in his home although we knew it might be a short time until Dad's own health breakdown would leave us no alternative with his living arrangement. Already, his attempts to cook and clean were totally unsafe. But for the moment, I turned to the local home health agency for assistance.

After filling out a stack of papers to change the aide's services to fit Dad's criteria instead of Mother's, she began a three-morning-a-week schedule to help with his cooking, cleaning, and laundry. The physical and mental strain of Mother's problems, coupled with his own physical limitations, had exhausted Dad. When I approached him about moving to the nursing home with Mother, he shook his head and answered, "I've got to have some rest." At the time, I did not understand how totally he held himself responsible for Mother's care and well-being. Nor did I fully realize the stress her demands had placed upon him.

Within a few days, Dad had accepted the aide's help with household chores. However, his personal hygiene was another matter. Although he did not require assistance, I explained that it was safer for him to bathe when someone was in the house. But he proved his independence by taking his shower the evening before the aide's visit.

While we worked out the details of household help, we counted down the days before Mother's move to the nursing center. The evening before her transfer, Diane and I told her the plan. She cried and shook her head in defiance. We both dreaded the next morning.

A MESSAGE IN A DREAM

Returning home, I unlocked my door in time to catch the ringing phone. My son's voice from his apartment in California came through loud and clear. I unleashed my despair in leaving Mother alone in a nursing home. I thought his nurse's training would give him words of comfort. I should have known better!

With his objective, sometimes cold, bedside manner, Tim had a way of cutting to the core of the problem. "Give it up, Mother," he said. "You have to let someone else carry some of this responsibility."

Tears welled up behind a huge lump in my throat. There was no one else to administer my parents' affairs—or so I thought. I had to end our phone conversation without responding.

I stumbled to my bed, hoping to pull up the covers and shut out the world for at least a few hours. Heavy sleep settled over my tired limbs and aching head. Sometime during the black of night, a dream startled me awake.

Usually, my dreams are fleeting images, gone when my eyes open. But this one remained clear—almost tangible—as I sat in bed clutching my knees to my chin. Scenes played over and over in vivid detail, etching a message in my brain.

In my dream-sleep state, my daughter Suzanne drove Mother, Daddy, and me down a twisting highway to the lake. Ever so quietly with no warning, she headed the car over the edge of the road and into the still wetness. As water rushed inside the windows, I saw Suzanne gliding with no effort to the silvery surface. Mother and Dad clutched my arms as a silent tow pulled us under, deeper and deeper into the watery blackness.

My helplessness to save them—and myself—engulfed me in the darkness. Tim's words, the same ones my husband and daughters had used for weeks, were underscored in the sobering dream. I knew I could not continue to carry the total load of my parents' care. The truth zipped through my thoughts like a shooting star against a blackened sky. *I can't save Mother and Dad from the progression of age. In trying to do so, I'm going under with them.*

I awoke with the same sadness that had wrapped me like a damp shawl morning after morning for many weeks. But recalling the dream's message, I had a renewed sense that I had done my best for Mother and Dad. Now I had to go on living, making choices other middle-aged people make, and meeting the needs of my own family. For a fleeting moment, the heavy cloud of guilt parted, releasing its smothering threat.

Oh God, I'm trusting you! I will hide beneath the shadow of your wings until this storm is past.

Psalm. 57:1 TLB

Chapter Four

A NEW KIND OF HOME

My sister and I made light conversation on the drive from the hospital to the nursing home, pointing out the silky, white petals of dogwoods spreading their limbs over winter's brown carpet. Mother had always loved our Ozark hillsides.

But on that dismal spring day, she stared straight ahead, her expressionless eyes fixed on the black ribbon of curving highway.

She uttered no sound as we entered our hometown and passed within a block of her home. So many memories of turning down that street. Good memories going back to when the school bus dropped me off on late winter nights following out-of-town basketball games.

Wrapped in a heavy coat, fingers and toes frozen numb, I had taken brisk steps toward the light in my bedroom window. I knew before cracking open the front door and slipping inside that Mother had turned down and warmed my bed with a low setting on the electric blanket.

Cold raindrops and a sharp wind hanging onto a remnant of winter mirrored the bleak likelihood that Diane and I would ever again experience those coming-home times, especially the tantalizing smells of mother's pot roast and fudge brownies.

A NEW PLACE TO LIVE

On this day, we turned our attention to a new kind of home—an institution, to be sure, but a home where we believed Mother would receive love and care. We didn't know her thoughts in her semi-confused state, but we coped with our own sense of loss for a stage of our lives that would never be again.

Parking under the nursing home's canopy, kind and gentle hands helped us lift Mother to the wheelchair. We squeezed her arm, trying to direct her attention to the spacious lobby. But vacant eyes, twisted bodies propped with pillows in reclining chairs, and rambling conversations of the residents lined up to see "the new lady" distracted from the seagreen carpet and matching wallpaper.

The social coordinator wheeled Mother to a room, cheerful with blue striped walls and matching drapes. She buried her head in her hands and cried, not noticing the decorator touches that usually caught her eye.

After she was situated in bed, we both gave her hugs and promised we would return later with Daddy. From her tightened lips, she mustered a faint, husky question: "Why did you put me here?" Her first intelligible words in two weeks.

Seeing her lying helpless against stark white sheets, guilt swept over me. I knew we had done our best for Mother, but the beautifully decorated room had unfamiliar walls, pictures, and chairs instead of the comfortable furnishings Mother and Dad had accumulated for more than fifty years in their home.

BACK TO REALITY

While I swam in a river of self-reproach, Diane brought me back to the tasks at hand. "We have a stack of papers to sign, clothes to label, and financial arrangements to meet," she said, understandably anxious to clear up our business and return to her family.

Mother had no comprehension of the agencies we had met and the business we had conducted to get their finances and household help in order. But those details proved minor compared to the emotional upheaval of knowing that some of the steps we took set our parents on a course we could not alter.

As the primary caretaker, I legally signed Mother into the nursing home. No matter how much I disliked the role, at that moment, I became her boss. She could not leave the facility unless I signed for her to go home or to another institution.

PREPARED FOR LONG-TERM POSSIBILITIES

Several years prior to our long-term-care dilemma, Mother and Dad had deeded their house and real estate to my sister and me. We thought we had planned well as far as holding onto their home in case one of them needed nursing-home care. Knowing their savings would not cover the cost of a private-pay resident, we applied at our State Office of Human Resources for assistance. But we learned that any resources Mother and Daddy had together—savings accounts, certificates of deposit, life insurance policies, or anything of monetary value—counted as assets for both of them.

"In other words, your dad must spend every resource down to a minimal amount before your mother can qualify for state aid," the man behind the desk had told us.

My sister and I sat in shocked silence because the allowed amount left barely enough for existence and nothing for any major expenses such as extra medications, the breakdown of a household appliance in their home, or the deductible for a hospital stay. We also learned that assets had to be transferred or divided at least two years prior to a request for assistance*. Mother and Dad had always pooled their so-

*Regulations for Medicaid, medical assistance to needy people whose income is low or medical expenses are too high to afford health care, may vary from state to state. Medicaid often supplements Medicare.

cial security checks in a joint account. All savings Dad had carefully put back for emergencies had both their names listed as owners.

Mother's burden of adjustment was heavy. But the decisions we faced, along with their awesome responsibilities, overwhelmed me. Looking down the road, we knew that a nursing-home lifestyle was inevitable for both parents. Dad could manage for a while with the home care I had arranged, but his own health hung precariously. At any moment, we could be moving him to the same facility.

We talked over the financial problems with him and decided to liquidate his resources as quickly as possible. Drawing on his thirty years experience as an insurance agent, he stubbornly clutched his life insurance policy. We explained that we needed the money to spend while he and Mother lived; not to squabble over after they were gone. Reluctantly, he agreed.

A prepaid burial policy is one asset a person in our state can own and not count as a resource. Before Diane left for Texas, we planned our parents' funerals, covering the expenses with cash from Dad's insurance policy. Sitting in the funeral director's office, we made harsh, yet practical, decisions. Daddy supported us, but Mother's state of mind could not take in the discussion of arrangements for their burials.

After Diane's departure, I set up a plan for spending their savings down to the allowed sum for a couple. Trying to project their needs for the next few years, I purchased clothing, a television for Mother's nursing-home room, and replacements for some of their outdated appliances at home. I established individual checking accounts, with their social security checks automatically deposited each month. The private-pay nursing-home fee also cut into their funds.

DETERMINATION ON THE HOME FRONT

While I dealt with financial matters, Mother in strong defiance pronounced daily in silent words that she would return home. Trying to maintain her former lifestyle as closely as possible—and appeasing my own guilt at the same time—I gathered up her soiled clothing rather than sending it through the nursing home's laundry.

In between monitoring his home health aides and checking on my own household, I drove Dad to the home for daily visits. With his poor hearing and Mother's whispered speech, their communication was limited to hand holding. The rest of the family and the nursing-home staff managed to read her lips, but Dad's weak eyes would not permit him to pick up on anything she pantomimed.

Dad and I were also anxious for Mother's physical therapy to continue. The nursing home lacked equipment, so I set up my stationary bicycle in her room and explained to the nurses how she sat in a chair behind the back wheel in order to reach the pedals.

A COMIC TRAGEDY IN THE MAKING

The second day, a nurse met me in the hallway. "Your mother can't ride that bicycle," she said. "I called in the entire staff to hold her up and she just can't ride it."

My hopes spiraled downward. "Has she regressed that much?" I asked.

The nurse continued to describe her lack of motor control. I was shocked to hear she could not pedal the bicycle when she had done so only the day before leaving the hospital.

The nurse shook her head. "She can't sit on that bicycle. She's as limp as wet pasta."

"Sit on the bicycle?" I questioned, the impact of what she said suddenly making sense. "Of course, she can't sit on the bicycle seat!"

I laughed at the image of three nurses and six aides trying to hold Mother on the bicycle and coordinate her feet to the pedals.

Poor Mother! The humor was bittersweet. With her lack of voice, she could not tell them. And they had never seen anyone sit in a chair to pedal a bicycle. After Mother and I demonstrated our procedure, she started a new trend in exercise for the nursing center.

SHARING SPACE

The next day, the social coordinator greeted us. "Your mother has a new roommate," she said. "I think it's best for her to have someone else in her room."

You don't know my mother, I thought, drawing a deep breath before entering her room. Although I knew the private room status had been temporary, I had hoped she would have a few more days to adjust.

Mother's swollen, red eyes met mine as Dad followed me through the doorway. She gestured that the woman's belonging were all over the floor. I noted only one bag near the bathroom door. But reasoning with Mother proved futile. I pulled the curtain separating her bed from the roommate's, clicked on the TV, and tried to divert her attention. Nothing penetrated her near-hysterical state. Over and over, she mouthed the words: "I want to go home!"

BATTLE LINES DRAWN

In desperation, I asked: "Mother, can you walk to the bathroom?"

She shook her head.

"Can you talk? Take your own medicine?"

Again, she answered in the negative.

"You can't go home until you can walk, talk, and take care of yourself," I said on that Friday afternoon. I believed with all my heart the feats I outlined were beyond her capabilities. But by Saturday, Mother walked down the hall holding to her metal walker. Her words sounded stronger.

On Sunday, she walked to the lobby and the dining room, assisted only by her cane. Her voice returned to its normal volume. I reflected on what the neurologist had said, ". . .possibly, psychological."

Mother's turnaround erased the misgivings I had had with him and the hospital staff. As they had predicted, she did things I thought were impossible.

KEEPING MY PROMISE

When Dad and I visited each day, her conversation focused on an angry determination to return home. Although I saw her improvement, past experiences told me that Mother could not function again in her own house. Taking medication in its proper dosage was in itself a major drawback.

I recalled her criticism of the health aide's cooking and laundry skills. Her falls. And weekends and evenings when there were no aides.

Dad sat stoically on a couch in the nursing home lobby while Mother raged. He had never in his life said "no" to her; but then, he usually did not verbalize "yes" either. This time was no different. He said nothing to Mother nor to me as I drove him back to his home each day.

The staff said, "Give it time. She'll adjust." *You don't know my mother,* I thought again.

By that time, the roommate had been transferred to another facility. They had projected Mother would accept her, too, but she did not. And I knew she would not have, even if the woman had stayed.

"Stay away for a week," the staff suggested when Mother persisted in her campaign to return home. But I could not. Yet, I remembered giving similar advice to parents hanging around the classroom door, peeking inside to see if their child was crying.

Some nurses reported that Mother visited with residents and laughed aloud when we were not with her. I did not believe them any more than some mothers had believed me when I said their children interacted well until they saw them at the end of the school day.

Day by day, Mother's tears, like water dripping on limestone, wore away my resistance. The end of April drew near, time to commit payment for another month. I walked in alone one afternoon and spotted her on a couch in the lobby. When her eyes caught sight of me, she stamped her cane on the floor and stated: "I'm going home! I won't spend Mother's Day here."

Butting personalities with Mother was like clicking on a cassette tape in my head. Dozens of scenes—always the unpleasant ones—connected in an endless parade. My stomach quivered like a bowl of Jell-O. My skin felt prickly, all hot and cold at once. I didn't know whether to cry or to throw up—and most of the time during confrontations, I thought I might do both.

"Okay, Mother," I managed to reply in a tone belying my frustration. "If that's what you want, then I'll take you home."

I walked down the hall to report my decision to the nurse. "You're making a mistake," she told me. "You need to go home and leave her for two weeks. She'll adjust."

"You may be right," I answered. "But I told her she could return home when she learned to walk and talk again. I have no choice but to honor my promise."

With arrangements complete to move her the next day, I drove to their home to tell Dad to expect her. He gave no support to my decision, but raised no objections either. I made yet another appointment with the county's home health services to rearrange the aide's schedule to accommodate Mother. By that time, the secretary had moved my parents from program to program so often that she did not ask any questions before shoving a handful of papers at me. After another evaluation, we established a five-day-a-week routine that included help for both Mother and Dad.

Let us not become weary in doing good, for at the proper time we will reap a harvest if we do not give up.

GALATIANS 6:9 (NIV)

Chapter Five

HOMECOMING

On a bright May morning—in striking contrast to the drab day on which we had introduced Mother to the nursing home—the staff helped load her belongings into my van. I guided Mother down the sidewalk and buckled her into the van's passenger seat. With few words between us, I drove across town to her home, occasionly glancing sideways at her frail image reflected in the windshield.

A bit of hope framed with a bunch of "maybes" lifted my spirits. Maybe Mother will try harder this time. She wants so desperately to live at home. Maybe she is stronger now. Maybe she'll accept her limitations and allow the aide to handle the household chores. Maybe, maybe . . .

The home health aide, followed by Dad in his stiff-legged gait, greeted us. Mother made her entrance like a queen checking out her subjects. As she took a grand tour, her hands lovingly touched chairs, pictures, and keepsakes on the tables.

"It's so good to be home," she said over and over. My reservations in exchanging a skilled nursing facility for part-time home health care dwindled as I watched the happiness in her eyes.

SETTLING IN

For the next two days, Mother slipped into a routine. The aide helped her with a daily bath, did laundry and prepared food for the evening meal. She made an extra casserole for weekends. Volunteers from the local "Meals on Wheels" delivered hot lunches. A housekeeper came weekly to do heavy cleaning. The yard man mowed and clipped. And the county health services sent a nurse to periodically check Mother's vital signs.

Since an aide cannot dispense medicine, I set up daily dosages in marked bottles. Some peace began to fill the crannies of my mind, occupied for months by the recurring question: "What am I going to do with Mother and Dad?"

But within seventy-two hours of Mother's return home, her emotions broke like a torrent of floodwater bursting through a dam. She insisted on taking nonprescription medications. Tears fell down her cheeks as she said her family did not care about her. She refused to eat the aide's meals and claimed that her skills did not include operating the new laundry equipment.

A NEW WEEK WITH NEW PROBLEMS

The aide reported daily incidences of pills and capsules dropped on the floor unnoticed. She watched Mother place a metal pan in the microwave and a paper-napkin-covered dish in the electric range's oven. One day, she walked into the utility room in time to grab Dad by the neck of his shirt before he fell backwards out the door. She happened to be in the right place at the right time, but I suspected Dad's falls were more numerous than he disclosed.

Another day, I questioned him about an ugly, red scratch on top of his balding head. "I pinched Betty and she hit me with a Coke bottle," he answered, a mischievous grin turning up the corners of his mouth.

"Sure, Dad," I retorted, knowing that pinching a woman was about the last thing to enter my dad's mind even when he was a young and spry man.

The aide chuckled when I related the incident, but neither of us knew what had happened to his head. And he stuck fast to his story. I found out long after the scratch had healed that he had squatted to tie Mother's shoes and could not regain his balance when he stood. His legs still bent, he had staggered around the living room until he hit his head on the brick fireplace.

A COLLISION OF WILLS

But while the aide laughed at Dad's excuses, Mother's lack of cooperation used up her patience. Knowing she had requested a transfer to another case, I pointed out to Mother that she had entered a stage of life where she could not safely do the things she once did on a routine basis. But by accepting the help we offered, she could manage to stay in her home and live comfortably—for a while.

She gripped the arms of her recliner and screamed: "I want to be my own boss! Just go on and live your life and let me live mine."

"I can't do that, Mother," I answered, my voice escalating to a pitch above hers. "Because I would barely get home and you'd call me for something you need. Against my better judgment, I brought you home from the nursing center because you wanted to come. I've done the best I can to arrange for your care, but if you won't cooperate, then you will go back."

Mother shook her head and clenched her jaw. "I will never, never go back to the nursing home," she said.

"Then you have no choice. Let the aide do her job," I said, my insides shaking from the emotional encounter. "And if you turn one knob on the cookstove," I added, determined to make my final stand, "I'll remove the heating element and carry it in my purse!"

While Mother and I locked horns verbally, Dad slumped in his chair. Although he understood her attitude toward the aide meant we might lose her services, he neither supported me nor defended Mother. As I left their house, I noticed he rubbed his right arm and grimaced in obvious pain.

Anxious to put some distance between me and my parents, I headed for my home. I had made my speech and issued my ultimatum. But what good would it do? Mother had never listened to me. And Dad sitting there, flexing his shoulder and rubbing his arm—I wondered what was next. The same question dogged my steps: *What can I do to ease the pain of this most difficult stretch of my parents' walk in life?*

My answer again came from God's word.

Commit everything you do to the Lord. Trust Him to help you do it and He will.

PSALM. 37:5 (TLB)

CHAPTER SIX

A WEARY JOURNEY BEGINS

Dad sat on the examination table in the neurosurgeon's office, his frail legs swinging off the side. His humped shoulders twitched with a pain he tried to rub from his right arm. The doctor slapped X rays on a lighted panel and nodded his head before turning to Dad. "Mr. Ramsey, push against my hand as hard as you can," he said. Dad's once-stout arms that had lifted barrels of gasoline when he worked as a truck driver offered little resistance to the doctor.

"I'm going to prescribe two weeks of therapy," he continued. "But if the pain persists, you will need surgery to correct this pinched nerve."

"Surgery," I gasped. "Can his heart stand surgery?"

"He won't have any choice," the doctor answered.

I ushered Dad from the doctor's office and headed my van toward our home, seventy miles north of the city. Conversations between us seldom centered on problems. We chatted about politics, church, and television programs.

Dad called the TV personalities who daily flickered across the screen by their first names. A casual observer would have thought Johnny Carson, then the host of NBC's *Tonight Show* and Ralph Emery, a well-known announcer for the Nashville Network, were coming to dinner. *Surgery* hung like a flashing red light in my mind, but neither of us spoke the word aloud.

A STOPGAP MEASURE

Starting the next morning, I drove Dad to the therapist's office on a daily schedule. She tenderly exercised his neck, shoulder, and arm. For an hour following the visits, the pain retreated, only to return with a vengeance.

Into the second week the therapist said, "You need to contact his doctor. His heart can't stand this kind of pain much longer."

THE SURGERY OPTION

A few days later, surgery was scheduled. Dad and I went to the same hospital where nine months earlier he had received his pacemaker. We settled into a room while my husband set up our travel trailer in a nearby park so I would have "room and board" during Dad's hospital stay.

At home, I had engaged a friend to stay overnight for the entire week with Mother. With the aide's daily visits and her noon meals delivered, only a few hours in the afternoons were not covered.

The nursing staff paraded in and out of Dad's room with more regularity than I had expected on any other floor of the hospital. I began to relax—until the second morning. A battery of X rays were scheduled to determine the extent of his nerve damage. Arriving at the hospital about an hour early, I walked into an empty room.

"He's already been taken to X ray," the nurse said. "You can wait here."

"No, I want to see the doctor," I answered and hurried for the elevator. As I rounded a corner in the long corridor leading to the waiting room for radiology, I spotted Dad's gurney. His legs dangled off the end. *What a strange position for an X ray*, I thought. When I reached his side, he babbled about going to the bathroom and pointed toward a doorway. I immediately recognized that he had been sedated and if I had not appeared, he might have landed on the floor.

Before I could question anyone about why he had been left alone in a hallway, a well-dressed gentleman rushed to his side, holding a urinal. Obviously, he was not a nurse nor a technician. With no explanation of how he had fallen heir to Dad's problem, he wheeled him into a room for privacy. I never saw the man again.

But the scene added to dozens of others: Dad trying to put an evening meal on the table and accidentally knocking Mother's walker across the kitchen floor. Dad staggering halfway across a room each time he stood to his feet. Dad topping a sandwich with a slice of molded cheese because he could not see or smell spoilage. Just one more incident gnawing the edges of my mind with the same question: *What can I do to keep Mother and Dad safe and happy?*

THE IMMEDIATE PROBLEM

Following the X rays, the neurosurgeon came out and explained the surgery he would perform later in the afternoon. I followed the orderly pushing Dad's gurney to his room, keeping an eye out for any attempt from him to get up without assistance. Although he had been taking care of his needs at home, Dad was a fall waiting to happen, even without sedation.

The hours during surgery dragged. My fingers pushed a needle in and out of fabric, creating a design with bright-colored thread. But my thoughts raced between Dad lying in the operating room and Mother at home waiting for my call. When the doctor walked into the waiting room, I clasped my husband's hand while my eyes traced the surgeon's face.

"Your dad did fine," he said with a smile that relieved my anxiety. "He will be in recovery a short while before returning to his room." Then he explained his procedure for a cervical fusion—grafting bone from the hip and fusing it on both sides of the neck vertebrae so that it no longer rotated and pinched the nerve. "The hip will give him more problem than the incision in the neck," he said. "But we'll have him walking tomorrow."

POST-OP PLANS

I requested a recliner so I could spend the night and settled in to wait for Dad's return to his room. The orderlies pushed him down the hallway, his arms waving and his fingers pointing as he once again tried to stop them at every doorway to use the bathroom.

I looked at James. "It's going to be a long night."

But by late afternoon, Dad's alertness returned. The nurses ordered a bed monitor that went off like a five-alarm fire alert every he tried to get up. After Dad had eaten his supper, I felt comfortable to join my husband for a night's rest at our trailer.

The next day, James returned home to manage our business, and I started my daily routine at the hospital. As the doctor promised, the nurses had Dad on his feet. Watching his stooped body jerk down the hallway, his frail hands grasping a walker, I overheard him say, "I walked good before this surgery." I shook my head at the nurse.

How is he going to manage at home? I tossed out the question like a boomerang and the answer came back: *I don't know.*

BEDSIDE TALKS

During the daylight hours, I sat by Dad's bedside, talking when he was awake, penning story ideas in my notebook when he napped. He told me about school activities in his rural community and what kind of merchandise he and his dad had stocked in their general store.

One afternoon, our conversation turned toward his present life at home. A few years earlier, my parents had undergone a major remodeling of their house. I had sketched out my idea for an additional bathroom, adjoining Dad's bedroom. The plan suited them both and Dad okayed the builder's bid.

"I've never added anything to our house that I've enjoyed as much as that shower in my bathroom," Dad said from his hospital bed. A silent skirmish played between us—me wrestling with the decision that could mean he would never use his shower at home again, and Dad desperately poking my conscience with barbs of innocent words.

MEANWHILE BACK AT HOME . . .

In the middle of the afternoon only two days after Dad's surgery, I answered the phone by his hospital bed to hear Mother's voice saying: "I have to see the doctor—now!"

"What's the problem?" I questioned.

"This headache," she answered, stating that her older sister and a cousin who lived next door were both there. "They think I need to go to the doctor, too. It's going to be a terrible night. I already know I won't sleep a wink."

"Mother, I'm eighty miles away in a hospital with Dad," I said. "I can't get you to the doctor. You said you've taken Tylenol. Give it time to work. And the lady who stays with you will be there in another hour."

I cut our conversation short and dialed my husband. "Would you go by and check on Mother?" I requested.

He called back within an hour to report that there was no crisis—only three little ladies in an emotional whirlwind. In his firm and objective manner, he calmed the situation. "But your mother is calling someone to stay with her every afternoon," he said. "She says she can't be alone."

I stayed with Dad at the hospital each evening until he finished his meal. Then I headed for the trailer park that was beginning to be a home away from home. Crawling into my bed, the strange city sounds—a passing train, heavy traffic on the parallel interstate, the beep of a forklift at a nearby heavy machinery plant—kept company with the question in my head. *How can I take care of Mother and Dad?*

CARE-PLAN OPTIONS

Back and forth I weighed out the alternatives. James matter-of-factly stated that Dad had to go to the nursing center. A nurse suggested that I could arrange a bedside commode and a walker by his bed so he could manage for himself. Dad, on the other hand, asked my teenage nephew to spend two weeks with him.

"You can sleep with me and help me to the bathroom and to the kitchen," he suggested to Brent.

What to do? What to do? I prayed, questioned, and thought aloud. The end of the week when Dad would be dismissed approached rapidly. Daily, I watched him struggle with a walker, losing his balance unless a nurse held his arm. I knew someone would not always be at home to hold him up. And I also knew the demands Mother made on him—demands he tried to meet even if he had to crawl.

With the doctor's approval, I checked at the nursing home where Mother had lived two months earlier. They had a space for Dad.

Watching his unsteady gait as a nurse guided him down the hallway, I believed there was no other choice. I confronted Dad, outlining my plan to transfer him to the skilled nursing center. With an air of defeat, but offering no resistance, he agreed. Remembering my experience with Mother, I did not promise he could go home when he could walk. But we both knew that is what he planned.

PLAYING THE SCENE AGAIN

Once again, I drove past the street leading to our home place. Dad showed little emotion as I eased the van under the nursing home's covered driveway. With assistance from the staff, we settled him into the same room Mother had occupied. I unpacked his bags and marked ARLIE RAMSEY on his clothing. "You rest with a nap, Dad," I said. "I'll bring Mother for a visit this afternoon."

He gave a slight smile as I waved good-bye.

Now that Dad had around-the-clock care, I turned my attention once again to Mother. The friend staying with her agreed to continue on a temporary basis. Understanding that she needed some time off, I found another lady to come in a couple of nights a week. Although their pay for sitting was well below an hourly minimum wage, the amount exceeded what I knew my parents could budget for an extended time. Little by little, I tried to point out to Mother that the time was coming for her to think about alternate living arrangements.

A NEW PLAN

One afternoon, standing in her kitchen, the scenario exploded between us. "Mother, you and Dad can no longer take care of yourselves in this house," I said. "You have to plan where and how you're going to live so that you can have the care you need."

She planted her feet firmly on the linoleum and steadied her hand on the kitchen sink. "I'll stay by myself. I won't have anyone to sleep over," she said.

"You won't even stay by yourself in the afternoons," I argued. "Wouldn't it be better if you moved to the nursing home with Dad so you could be together?"

"No," she screamed back at me.

"All I'm asking, Mother, is that you begin to think about what you're going to do," I said. "This arrangement can't work for any length of time. You and Dad are going to have to make a change."

SMALL CONCESSIONS

The month wore on. Dad made a friend at the home—a dignified gentleman who had suffered a broken neck and was totally confined to a wheelchair. He and Dad shared a table in the dining room and enjoyed discussing the man's career in banking and Dad's experiences in insurance. However, Dad's refusal to let us move his TV into his room underlined his subtle defiance: *Don't get me too comfortable.*

One day he mentioned a pro-baseball game score. "Someone changed the channel and I didn't get to see the end of the game," he said.

"Where did you watch the game?" I asked.

"In the lobby," he replied.

On the next visit, James and I moved his own television into his room. "Now Dad, you can watch ball games whenever you want and no one will change the channel," I told him.

My speech to Mother made more impact than I had thought. She approached Dad about moving herself to the nursing home. But he sat tight-lipped. She talked to some of the staff and looked at a room on a different hall which would be available for the two of them. But when she tried again to talk to Dad, he stared at the wall or changed the subject to something about a television program.

Mother threw herself into a panic trying to weigh out the decision of moving to the nursing home. "If he'd only talk to me," she said. "If only he'd go and look at the room."

One day, she tottered down the hallway to check out the room again and I confronted Dad. "What do you plan to do?" I questioned.

"I thought I'd get back to walking good and go home," he said.

"Dad, you're walking as good as before. But nothing else has changed. Mother still doesn't like the aide's work; she can't take medicine by herself. You are unsteady on your feet; you can't see. Look at the number of hospital visits you and Mother have had in the past year. Even if you go back home, it's only going to be until the next crisis—maybe a few weeks, a month. Then you're going to be right back here."

I watched for any sign of emotion on his face. But his dimmed eyes looked straight ahead.

"Wouldn't it be better for both of you to move now while you can visit with each other, talk to the other residents, and be up and around?

"Won't you please talk to Mother about this? She's agonizing over this decision and you sit there not saying a word to her."

"What about our finances?" he asked. "I didn't want to talk to her until I knew if we could financially make the change."

"Yes, Dad. I have everything arranged," I said, outlining how I had spent their assets—pre-paying funeral plans, buying clothing, and purchasing other items they needed. "Talk to Mother and give her some help."

Dad did not talk to Mother. But he reluctantly accepted her moving to the nursing home. "Because she can't take care of herself," he said.

"Because my husband cannot take care of himself," Mother told her friends and the nursing home staff. "He wanted me there with him—until he can get well and we can return home." And every now and then, she would slip and say," . . . until he can take care of me again."

A NEW HOME

My daughters and I selected personal items—two recliners, paintings, family pictures, a lamp, and knickknacks—to decorate my parents' new room. The staff approved my purchase of new drapes and matching bedspreads. We moved their telephone with the same number they had had since the dialing system had been installed in our small town. The room looked as much like home as possible.

Then we went to work emptying the refrigerator and cupboards and closing their house. I had the water and gas disconnected, but left the electricity on so we would have lights when we needed to change out their clothes for the seasons.

As I locked the door, finality mixed with relief. My parents had constant care in their new home, but the key turning in the lock of their house represented the end of their independence. Nothing would ever be the same again for them—or for me.

But even so, you love me! You are holding my right hand! You will keep on guiding me all my life with your wisdom and counsel.

PSALM 73: 23-24 (TLB)

Chapter Seven

FIRST STEPS DOWN DAD'S ROUGHEST ROAD

"Come quick!" Mother's voice, cracking with sobs, came through the phone line. "They're taking everything I've got."

I dropped the vacuum cleaner and jumped in my van, speeding on two wheels to the nursing home. When I walked in, Mother sat on the edge of her bed crying; Dad had collapsed in his recliner.

What on earth is happening?" I asked.

"They came in and took everything away," Mother explained. "My hair spray, Aspercreme, Preparation-H, everything."

"Mother, you know the rules. You can't have aerosol cans or medications in your room. But they didn't take it away. They have everything at the nurses' desk. You can ask for it."

"They won't give it to me," she retaliated. "It's like a prison. I hate this place!"

Through her tirade, Dad sat with his head in his hands. I looked from one to the other. Never had I seen two more miserable people. And never had I felt so helpless. The past two years keeping them in their home had been a nightmare. I had thought that having around-the-clock care would alleviate some of the problems. But daily life in the nursing home played more like a horror movie.

From the day Mother moved into the home, Dad's personality had changed. He bitterly complained that the food was rotten and even signed a birthday card to my sister: "From the jailhouse."

Not knowing what to say to comfort them, I sat on Dad's bed listening to Mother's complaints. Suddenly Dad looked up and said: "Our only hope is that we won't live long."

In retrospect, I do not believe Dad calculated his words to put me on a guilt trip. Nevertheless, his statement pierced my heart like a white-hot dagger.

"I can't believe you would say something like that to me, Dad," I responded, the tears welling up quickly. All I could think of was one of our conversations in his hospital room.

A WALK IN HIS DAD'S SHOES

One afternoon, he had recalled his desperation when his dad—my sweet, gentle Pap-pa—had to be placed in a nursing home. There was no room in the facility in our community, so arrangements were made in a town forty miles away. Pap-pa hated every minute he was away from his home.

As Dad described the situation, I recalled that my children were small at that time, preventing me from making regular visits to the home. But I wrote a note to him daily. However, the nurses reported that he cried when they read them, so I stopped writing. As Daddy talked, it seemed so far away.

But his words interrupted my thoughts. "One Sunday when we visited, Papa told me I had to get him out of there," he said. "I didn't know what I was going to do. So I went home and called my sister Zula, and asked her to talk to him. And she did."

Yes, Dad, I thought, applying his words to my present dilemma about his care. *But I don't have a 'Zula' to call on.* When Dad experienced firsthand my Papa's hopeless feelings, he seemed to have forgotten his own cave of despair in dealing with his parent. Indeed, none of us understood until we faced my parents' move to a nursing facility.

MEANTIME, IN THE PRESENT

Nevertheless, his harsh words cut to the center of my heart. I fled their room before my anger boiled over. At the moment, my indignation at their apparent lack of appreciation for what I considered my sacrificial efforts in taking care of their needs blinded my understanding that Dad had lost control of his life. He assumed the role of martyr, the only psychological defense mechanism he had ever learned to use in life's battles.

Down the hall, I encountered the head nurse and asked her what had happened in their room that morning. She explained that the nursing staff periodically checks residents' drawers and closets for items such as aerosol cans and medications. "We have some residents who would drink mouthwash or cologne," she said. "And the rules about these items in their rooms are mandated from the state. We have no choice."

Once again, she suggested that I stay away for two weeks. "I can't do that," I answered.

"They're piling guilt on you," she said.

"I'll handle it," I replied, allowing my "superwoman" self-image to dominate any decisions about my parents' well-being.

But I didn't handle it. The relief I had anticipated in knowing that someone dispensed their medication properly and watched to see if they had fallen turned into a turmoil gripping me like a vise. Most days as I drove to the nursing home, waves of nausea heaved my stomach and tears of frustration burned my eyes.

LEANING ON A FRIEND

When our dear friend, Mr. Earl, as we called him, moved two doors down the hall from Mother and Dad, I hoped their longstanding friendship from church would boost my parents' sagging spirits. Mr. Earl's heart was failing, and his weakened body could not withstand surgery. But whatever his body lacked in strength, his spirit compensated with a steadfast faith.

He joined Mother and Dad in the dining room, adding to the small circle of friends around two tables. "You know the doctors only gave Mr. Earl six months to live," I said to Dad, not wanting his friend's impending death to come as a shock.

"Yes, he told me," Dad answered. "Earl's ready."

I quietly thanked God for the bond of friendship between two aging men. *Dear God, let their strong faith undergird each other,* I prayed.

On days when Mr. Earl's strength peaked, he mingled with residents and staff, spreading his optimism and cheer. I marveled when he asked his sons to sell his house and dispose of the tools from his woodworking shop. I prayed his example of turning loose of material possessions might encourage Mother and Dad to accept the nursing facility as their new home.

"Earl has no choice," Dad said, acting as though his friend's decision came without conflict. "His children live far away; his wife is dead, and he can't stay by himself."

"He doesn't like it here either," Mother added. In their minds, Mr. Earl's situation bore no similarity to theirs, except in their mutual distaste for the food.

A STRANGER IN MY DAD'S SKIN

Trying to keep our family traditions as normal as ever for Mother's and Dad's sakes, I planned a get-together in honor of Dad's eightieth birthday. My husband barbecued ribs and I put together all the trimmings from potato salad to ice cream and cake. When I picked up my parents at the nursing center for their evening out, Dad carried a lump wrapped in a brown paper towel.

"What's that, Dad?" I asked.

"It's my burned biscuit from breakfast," he said. "I want all the family to see what they serve us up here."

"Hard as a brick," Mother added as she tottled down the hall leaning on her cane.

I peeked inside the wrapping, not believing the change in my dad's behavior. The biscuit was indeed browned, but not burned. And naturally, it was hard since it had been sitting on his bedside table since the morning meal.

That evening, Dad's decorated cake took a back seat to the biscuit he placed as a centerpiece on the table. When each family member arrived, he recounted the burned bread, the lack of bacon for breakfast, and the food that was cold when it was supposed to be hot and hot when it was supposed to be cold. I thought about the meager breakfasts he had prepared for years at home—toast, sometimes burned, and jelly or a bowl of cornflakes. I could not remember when my parents had cooked bacon or eggs, much less biscuits, for a meal.

Dad's voice interrupted my thoughts: "Cutting back," he said with a sarcasm unlike the Daddy I knew. "They can't afford to serve us bacon every day."

MORE CHANGES

A few weeks later, Mother mentioned that Dad could not keep food down.

"It's rotten," he said. "I can't eat it."

Their family doctor sent a young associate to check on him. On my next visit, Dad announced, "Dr. Jerk's been here."

"Who are you talking about?" I inquired.

"That new young doctor who doesn't know anything," he answered.

My dad had never intentionally called someone a derogatory name. I watched a sneer cover his face as he complained about how the young man did not even address himself when he entered the room. Then he used the title, Dr. Jerk, again.

"Dad, you cannot call your doctor a name like that," I responded.

"Well, just what would you call him?"

"He has a name. Don't ever let me hear you call him Dr. Jerk," I said with a tone I might have used several years earlier with one of my teenagers.

The problem with Dad's digestion did not improve. The nursing staff suggested a visit to his doctor's office. I watched while one of our doctor's associates—not the one Dad had labeled Dr. Jerk—listened to his complaints about the ". . . rotten food." He never felt of his abdomen, took a test, or checked him.

"You look like a man capable of making his own decisions," he said, patting Dad on the knee. "We'll fix you up with this new medicine and if you need me for anything, give me a call day or night." And he handed Dad his business card. I felt as though his words had stamped 'mean daughter who placed her father in a nursing home' on my forehead!"

Turning to me, he said, "I think he's depressed. We'll start with a low-dosage 'mood elevator,' then, if he doesn't improve, progress to a higher one."

The medication made no changes in either Dad's disposition or his digestion. Most days, he simply refused to eat because everything came back up. "It's this awful food," he told me over and over. "It's ruined my stomach."

After a few weeks, I requested a referral to a specialist in the city. We sat across a desk from the doctor while he quizzed Dad and made notes on a clipboard.

"How do you like living in the nursing home?" the internist questioned.

"I don't like it," Dad answered.

"Why are you living there? Can you take care of yourself at home?"

"Yes, I can do everything for myself at home," Dad replied. "But my wife can't take care of herself."

"Then what you are saying is that you could live at home but you can't take care of your wife at home," the doctor prodded.

"But it gets awful hard to take care of her in the nursing home," he stated.

I listened, recalling Dad's angry words a few weeks earlier, "I'm only hanging on because if I'm gone they will really mistreat your mother." The nurses had reported that Dad had taken up Mother's battles, often accompanying her to the nurses' station to demand a particular medication or treatment.

It's no different from when they were at home, I suddenly realized. Dad had always stood in the gap for Mother, and he couldn't release her care to anyone else—and she couldn't accept that he was no longer physically or mentally able to meet all her needs.

The doctor's voice ordering a battery of tests jarred me back to the present. We left his office for the radiology department.

My aunt had accompanied us for the appointment. We waited while they took Dad into an inner office, dressed him in a surgical gown, and dosed him with a contrast medication for the X rays. "The procedure should take only an hour," the technician stated.

When an hour and a half had passed, I inquired. "You may go back and visit with your dad," the receptionist said. "We're waiting for the contrast to go through his digestive tract."

I found Dad huddled on a hard, narrow bench in a tiny cubicle, waiting for someone to direct him to the X-ray room. Although he did not complain, I knew from the stress in his eyes that he was weary of that uncomfortable position. I questioned another technician about the delay.

He told me the procedure for the dye to trace through his system was taking much longer than expected. And he gave permission for Dad to dress and leave the office for lunch.

Relieved for any reprieve from the confines of his waiting space, Dad pulled on his shirt and pants. We drove to the mall and ate lunch.

When we returned, the radiologist completed the X rays. My apprehensions already aroused by the slow passage of the contrast liquid Dad had to drink, I waited to speak to the doctor. He reported a blockage in Dad's stomach that he projected to be scar tissue from ulcers.

I had never known my dad to suffer from ulcers, but the radiologist expressed surprise that he was not having even greater problems in digesting food. I kept the report to myself, but the next morning his internist phoned to say that Dad needed surgery immediately.

He scheduled the procedure within the next few days, explaining that if the opening in his stomach completely closed off, Dad could be facing an emergency situation. I questioned him about why our family doctor had not discovered this problem when I took him in earlier. The internist expressed that I should be tolerant of the first doctor.

"I, too, expected to find nothing on those tests," he answered. "I thought your dad suffered from depression. But we have to repair this problem quickly."

AN UNWILLING MESSENGER WITH AN UNWANTED MESSAGE

I walked in my parents' room at the nursing home and seated myself by Dad's chair. "Your doctor says you have to have surgery," I said, placing my hand on his frail arm. I explained about the blockage around the opening in his lower stomach. "He wants you to enter the hospital on Sunday and have the surgery on Monday."

Mother's hand covered her mouth. "No, he can't have surgery. I can't go through it again," she said between sobs that shook her body.

Ignoring Mother's distress, Dad's lower jaw twitched with emotion. "You planned to be away this weekend," he said. "You can't cancel your trip."

"I already have, Dad," I said. "Getting you 'fixed' is more important than going to a flea market 500 miles away. There will be other times for that."

Mother bordered on hysteria while Dad tightened his lips and stared at the wall. "I can't take it. I can't take it!" she went on.

With one eye on Dad, trying to gauge his emotions, I spoke sharply. "For goodness sakes, Mother. Dad is the one who's facing the surgery. I'm the one who has to stand by his bed. And all you can think about is that you can't take it? Get hold of yourself!"

She calmed for a moment and I reached for Dad's hand. "I'm going to call now and make the arrangements," I told him. "And I'll be back later to tell you exactly when we're leaving."

When I returned, I carried a notecard. "Mother, I don't know why this is happening to Dad; I know it's hard for you to face, too," I said. "But I've written a verse of scripture on this card. When you don't understand why things are happening, look at these words and remember that God is in control."

I opened the card and read:

For I know the plans I have for you," says the Lord. "They are plans for good and not for evil, to give you a future and a hope.

JEREMIAH 29:11 (TLB)

Chapter Eight

THROUGH THE VALLEY OF THE SHADOW OF DEATH

"Someone has to stay with me," Mother insisted.

"Someone is with you every hour of the day and night. You live in a nursing home," I answered, impatiently.

"But they don't care about me," she countered. "Some of the family has to stay while your Daddy is in the hospital."

I mentally clicked off Dad's necessities—pajamas, robe, and house slippers. I packed his bag and argued with Mother at the same time. "There will be someone to stay with you during Dad's surgery," I assured her. "But no one can sit here day and night. That's why you live in a nursing home. So there will always be someone to care for you.

"Dad will be fine. As soon as he comes from the operating room, I'll call you."

I gave her a hug and held back the tears as she kissed Daddy. With his failing heart, I knew full well that they might not see each other again in this life. But God had promised a future—not just to younger people, but to everyone. I held onto that promise as I guided Dad down the hallway to my waiting van.

Mr. Earl stepped from his room and touched my arm. "I'll watch over your mother," he said. "I'll do what I can to keep her spirits up."

Looking into the eyes of that gentle man, the image of his beloved wife flashed through my mind—Flo greeting people at the church door, visiting shut-ins, and smiling from her sick bed, encouraging those who visited her. Mr. Earl understood Mother's feelings in watching a mate suffer surgery, illness, and debilitating treatments.

"Thank you," I said, squeezing his frail and stooped shoulders. "You're a good friend."

James once again packed our travel trailer and pulled it to the park near the hospital. Dad and I followed its taillights over our two-lane county roads leading to the interstate.

We checked into a semi-private room and waited to meet the surgeon. Dad's roommate was a burly man from a town north of our home. His voice boomed against the hospital's sterile walls with a good-natured banter that Dad's near-deaf ears could pick up.

MEETING THE DOCTOR ON COMMON GROUND

By the time the surgeon introduced himself, Dad's spirits had risen. After explaining the surgical procedure and questioning him to make sure he understood the seriousness of the operation, the doctor put his hand on Dad's and asked: "Do you know Jesus?"

He had touched common ground. A grin spread across Dad's face. "I sure do!" he answered.

"Then let's pray about this surgery." The doctor voiced a simple prayer, placing himself and his patient into God's hands.

I followed him to the door. "Is my daddy going to be all right?" I asked.

"Keep your eyes on Jesus," he replied. "This is major surgery and there's always a risk." And he was gone.

THE LONG WAIT

Other family members joined me in the surgery waiting room. When the operation took an hour longer than projected, I anxiously waited for the doctor to appear. He finally called us to a small conference room.

"Your dad did fine," he said. "I removed forty percent of his stomach. We'll wait for a report from pathology to be sure, but I didn't see any signs of cancer."

"Thank you, God," I breathed.

THE BEDSIDE VIGIL

Everyone returned to their homes and I moved to the ICU waiting room for three days of irregular visits with Dad. His frail frame against sterile-white sheets was a mere shell of the man I knew. Tubes crisscrossed his body, connected to bags and jars that dripped input or caught output.

"He's making progress," the nurses assured me on each timed visit. But his glazed eyes, open but not seeing, did not match their optimistic reports.

One afternoon, I entered his light-filled corner cubicle. "Look at that squirrel," Dad said, pointing to the window ledge.

He was two floors off the ground with no trees near the building. But we watched squirrels anyhow.

In a few days, Dad was transferred to a private room on the eighth floor. He seemed more alert and I pointed out the couch that made a bed and a spacious desk with chair. "Look Daddy, I can sit right here and work while you get better."

Although I had been spending nights in my trailer while Dad stayed in ICU, I decided to spend his first night on the floor in his room. Spreading books and papers over the desk while keeping one eye on his pale face, I set to work on children's church curriculum, an assignment that had already received two extensions due to my parents' illnesses. My family discouraged me from taking on further work—and sometimes I questioned my obsession to keep on writing—but sitting in a hospital room surrounded by someone else's pain, the diversion provided my only link to the outside world.

During the night's darkest hours, Dad thrashed about in his bed. Clutching his side rails, he thought he bounced and jostled back and forth on an old school bus while traveling to the northern corner of our county. Recalling similar episodes with Mother in another hospital, I answered when he called old friends' names. "Steer it right over here," he insisted and became upset when I did not roll his bed along what he envisioned as rutted roads.

I rang for the nurse and we both tried to calm him. She administered a medication to induce some rest. But the confusion grew worse. Dad babbled nonsense and stared with wide-opened eyes throughout the remainder of the night. For the next two days and nights, he did not close his eyes.

Nearing exhaustion on the second night, I made up the extra bed and pulled it parallel to Dad's. With his side railing up, I reached through metal bars to grasp his leg while I tried to catch a few minutes sleep.

The days wore on. The projected two-week stay turned into three, then four weeks as Dad slowly progressed enough that I could leave him at night. James drove down on weekends to stay with me. One daughter and her husband brought Mother to visit. Another daughter, along with cousins, aunts, uncles, and friends, came and went.

DOWN A ONE-WAY ROAD WITH NO TURNAROUNDS

Pacing up and down the hospital corridors or sitting by Dad's bedside, I wrestled with other questions: *Should I cancel the supplemental medical insurance both my parents carried? With their bills processed under both Medicare and Medicaid, would they ever need the extra coverage?*

With health care providers filing bills to both services, I had also discovered that charges had been batted around for extended time periods without payment. It appeared to be some kind of political game for Medicaid to refuse to pay as long as there was the slightest chance that Medicare would pick up the tab. And vice versa.

I sought advice from the hospital's social services staff. A young man listened intently to my dilemma before dashing off to make phone calls and inquiries about what kind of needs were covered under the two systems. My main concern in canceling the supplemental policies came down to the question: *Will Mother and Dad ever leave the nursing facility?* As long as they lived there, they did not need the extra coverage. But if I canceled it, there would be no way to reinstate it at the current premium rate.

Day in and out, I argued the points in my head. If there was an outside chance either of them would ever live at home again, we would need the policy. On the other hand, I did not believe Mother and Dad could ever function outside an institutional setting. But the decision was mine. Dad was too ill for discussion. And Mother never comprehended financial matters, even when she was a young woman. Besides, there was no doubt in her mind that she would return to her home as soon as Dad came through this crisis.

I weighed the pros and cons as heavily as I had the decision to place Mother and Dad in a nursing home four months earlier. My heart cried "no," but my head said "yes." Listening to the social worker report his findings, I decided dropping the coverage was the only practical solution. But I agonized that I had taken another step that sealed my parents' fate to life in institutional care.

YANKING DAD UP WITH A BROKEN BOOT STRAP

From our eighth-story vantage point, I watched the autumn colors creep over the horizon line. Trying to interest Dad, I described the beauty, but his failing eyes could not see. And his defeated spirit refused to push his body to heal. His once-hearty appetite disappeared, and meal times became a dreaded chore with me coaxing him to down some Jell-O, and him clinching his lips after two bites.

"Don't you know they took out half my stomach?" he barked. "I can't hold it!"

One dark rainy day, Dad's skin tones matched the gray sky framed in the hospital window. When his breathing became labored, I called for his cardiologist.

With an order for increased oxygen, his breathing relaxed and I went downstairs to have lunch. As I entered the cafeteria, I heard the hospital intercom page Dad's doctor. Instinctively, I knew the patient was my dad. Turning on my heel, I rushed back to the elevator and stepped out on the eighth floor.

My intuition was right. Dad had taken a downward turn. I sat by his bed all afternoon, watching his ashen face, listening to his raspy breaths. His life hung in a balance, totally in God's hands. *Keep your eyes on Jesus*, I heard his surgeon's words. My eyes would have to be strong enough for both of us because, like a receding waterline on the lake in summer, Dad's will to live slowly seeped away.

By morning, the crisis had passed and once again, he improved. At the end of October, the doctors dismissed Dad back to the nursing center. Although I longed to return to my home, I dreaded facing the nursing center scene again.

A REUNION
TINGED WITH PAIN

Mother waited in the doorway. She patted his covers, hovered like a mother hen, and kept the call light on continuously requesting a nurse's assistance. Dad refused to talk, to eat, or to get out of bed. The doctors gave their go-ahead for him to resume a normal diet in smaller quantities. But he refused to try any foods he had previously liked. Each day he demanded grilled cheese sandwiches, which the dietitian placed on his tray for all three meals.

Our family planned Thanksgiving. Dad specifically ordered a two-inch square of turkey, a tablespoonful of dressing, and pecan pie. Nothing else. While Mother joined us for a festive meal, I filled a meager tray for Dad and delivered it to his room. When I returned to the home later with Mother, most of the food sat in cold lumps on his plate.

ONE CRISIS ON THE HEELS OF ANOTHER

By late evening, our phone rang. Mother's voice demanded: "Come take your dad to the hospital."

James and I rushed to the nursing home. Dad sat in his recliner, bent double with pain. Mother paced the floor in her small, shuffling steps, repeating over and over: "He has to go to the hospital."

The nursing staff believed Dad had an attack of gas. In fact, the head nurse had warned me about feeding him cornbread stuffing. "I'm not telling you he can't have it on Thanksgiving," she said. "But it's one of our more gassy foods."

My husband went to the cold-drink machine and bought a canned cola. We urged Dad to drink as much as possible. Within in a few minutes, he began belching and releasing some of the gas. We pulled him from the chair. With one of us holding each arm, we walked him up and down the darkened hallway. In less than an hour, the severe pain had subsided, and we tucked him back in bed.

But one crisis resolved into another. A week later, a nurse phoned. "I found your mother sitting on the floor about a half hour after you left this morning," she said. "She's not hurt, but she is disoriented."

I left my lunch preparations and drove to the home. For several hours, I sat by her bed, trying to keep her calm. She fought to get up, but did not know why. Her sentences came out nonstop, making no sense. By early evening, she had slipped into a comatose state. Her doctor ordered her transferred to the local hospital.

"Another mini-stroke," he diagnosed after running some tests. "This time, it looks as though the hemorrhage is at the base of the brain. I can't tell how she'll respond."

For three days and nights, I sat by Mother's lifeless form. My daughters took turns squeezing her hand and talking to her about incidents from their childhood. But there was no response.

MEANWHILE, THERE'S DAD . . .

At the nursing home, Dad sat in his chair, dissolving in tears when I told him that Mother was unconscious. Mr. Earl sat at his side, comforting and praying.

On the second morning, Dad's room filled with men from his Sunday-school class—faith-filled, praying men. They circled him with their love. "If your mother doesn't make it, it's not for lack of prayer," Dad said to me, his once, strong voice choking with emotion. "I've never heard men pray harder."

But Mother lay limp and fragile in her hospital bed. Nurses came and went, bathing her body, shampooing her curly white hair, tending to every need. Still she slept, never twitching even a finger.

With Christmas only two weeks away, I watched over her and sewed gifts for my family. The doctors gave me little hope for recovery. But one evening, friends dropped by her room. As we talked in low tones, Mother groaned and raised her arm. I went to her side and she slightly opened her eyes and tried to smile.

"Do you know who this is?" I asked, pointing to the friend standing behind me. In a raspy whisper, she drawled her name.

A SLOW COMEBACK

For the next week, confusion replaced Mother's deep sleep. As I spooned Jell-O and creamed soup into her mouth, she asked about Daddy. "He's at the nursing home. And you're in the hospital," I told her.

"Why doesn't he come to see me?" she asked in a faltering voice. "He has his car."

"No, Mother," I answered. "You and Dad gave your car to Brent. Daddy doesn't have a car now."

"He bought another one for twenty-five dollars," she said.

A WEEK BEFORE CHRISTMAS

Mother was dismissed from the hospital and transported back to the nursing center. Although the confusion remained, she slowly improved. Because she required extra help with eating and bathroom functions, the nursing staff placed her on a hall with additional aides. I wheeled her and Dad back and forth for visits.

Several days before Christmas, the nursing home entertained the residents with a party. Although Mother's mind still clouded, she looked forward to the activity.

"Dad, I want you to go to the party," I said.

He drew his face in a long frown that placed his chin close to his belt line. "What for?" he huffed.

"Because it's important to Mother."

I wheeled him into the dining room and rowed his chair next to hers. Mother grabbed his arm, only turning loose to clap her hands in time to the music. Dad crouched like a wild animal, his eyes darting around the room as though he looked for an escape.

The residents' families prepared a sumptuous buffet of holiday foods. Mother gobbled up everything I piled on her plate. Dad refused to even sip punch.

When I rolled him back to his room, he climbed into bed and pulled the covers tight under his chin. "The next time I hear they're having a party, I'm going to bed before it starts!" he grumbled.

A DIFFERENT CHRISTMAS

By Christmas Eve, Mother had moved back to the room she shared with Dad. My husband and daughters trooped in with gifts for them to open. Mother, always the one who loved presents, tore off the wrappings and exclaimed over the contents. Dad, looking like a skeleton with skin stretched taut, showed little emotion.

Nothing could ever replace the happier occasions when my parents opened their gifts under a tree in their own home. I could not remember a Christmas celebrated anywhere else. As sad as it was for Mother and Dad, it marked a passage of time for me and my children. A part of our lives had ended—scenes we would never recapture.

As the holidays ended and the gray wintry weather of January settled over our surrounding mountains, my parents' gloom spilled like black ink over every aspect of my life. They had no joy in each other, in my visits, or in living out their allotted time. The guilt of placing them in a nursing home crept over me like a drab, scratchy cloak.

Give your burdens to the Lord. He will carry them.

PSALM 55:22 (TLB)

Chapter Nine

A NEW TERROR

Mother lay flat on the examination table in a radiology unit thirty miles from our home. I overheard the doctor's words as he looked over the ghostly shadows hanging on a light box outside the door. "Malignant . . . needs immediate attention."

With determined strides, he entered the room to examine Mother. "Mrs. Ramsey, you have a lump in your left breast about the size of a grape," he said.

"I could feel it," Mother said, her calmness an opposite reaction from when I had announced Dad's impending abdominal surgery six months earlier. "And I want it out. When can I have it done?"

The soles of my pumps froze to the tile floor as I listened to the doctor's words. I hadn't expected this. Mother had called me in a frenzy a few days prior, demanding that I take her immediately to the doctor. "I've found a lump in my breast," she said.

"Have you shown it to the nurse?" I questioned, not alarmed because Mother routinely checked her body for bumps, spots, or bruises that neither I nor the nurses could find.

"She couldn't feel it," Mother replied. "But I know it's there."

Knowing there was no need to see a doctor until we had a mammogram, I phoned Mother's daytime nurse. She confirmed that she could not feel the lump, but suggested that I take her in for a routine checkup.

The doctor's voice addressing Mother jerked me back to the present. "The best thing is to take care of it before it spreads," he said. Gathering my wits, I followed him into the hallway.

"Mother has had several mini-strokes," I explained, remembering that only weeks before, she had hovered between life and death. "I don't know if she can withstand a surgery."

"Talk this over with your surgeon. He may prescribe something like a lumpectomy," the doctor said. "But it looks like cancer and you must not ignore it."

THE DREADED "C"

Cancer. The mere word, especially connected with the breast, struck chords of terror. Almost a year before to the exact date, my dear neighbor—more than dear, like my flesh-and-blood sister—had received the diagnosis: breast cancer.

Within six months, she was gone. My friend, ten days older than me, had shared dolls, dress-up clothes, and boyfriends. She had rocked and cuddled my children like her own. Now I heard the same awful words like a needle hanging on a phonograph record—breast cancer, breast cancer, breast cancer.

What must be going through Mother's mind? What can I say to ease her fear? Recalling the times when she had had a tiny skin cancer removed from her face and had refused to be seen in public for six weeks, I could only imagine what the loss of a breast would do to her.

Not cancer, Lord. Mother had always anticipated that any ache in her body would turn into the dreaded disease. I braced myself for her hysteria. But her composure remained intact as I slipped a blouse over her head. She announced the diagnosis to her sister, who sat in the waiting room. My head still reeling from the news, I helped Mother into the van and headed for a quick lunch. My hamburger chewed like shoe leather while she relished each bite. Eyeing me across the table, she said, "I'm not going to have chemotherapy."

"Mother," I exclaimed, venting my frustration with an open fist slammed on the tabletop. "Don't be ridiculous. We don't even know whether or not you'll need a mastectomy. Let's don't jump ahead to chemotherapy."

In my mind, I recalled the side effects from cancer treatments that I had witnessed in my friend. I did not believe Mother could face such an ordeal.

SETTING THE DATE

Within a few days, we made an appointment with Dad's surgeon, who agreed with the radiologist's diagnosis. "We can't be sure until we do the surgery, but it looks as though she does have a small breast cancer."

Mother accepted his words with no apparent apprehension. "How soon can we get it out?" she asked. We chose a date in mid-February.

"Your mother should be hospitalized less than a week," the surgeon said. I checked my own calendar. An annual writer's conference I had planned to attend was more than a month away. If things went well, I should get Mother back to the nursing home in time for me to go. Her confidence, bolstered by the doctor's reminder to ". . . keep your eyes on Jesus," eased my initial fears.

Once again, my husband pulled our trailer to the park while Mother and I checked into the hospital.

On the night before surgery, we got her settled and went out for dinner. When we returned to the hospital, Mother was sitting in a wheelchair at the nurses' desk, expressing fear in being alone. The nurse explained that she could not spend all of her shift in Mother's private room. Embarrassed by her demands, I acknowledged that I understood. But wheeling Mother back to her room, she complained of a scratchy throat.

"Some mouthwash to gargle might help," she said.

The nurse could not prescribe it without a doctor's order. "But I have no control over something you buy in the downstairs drug store and use yourself," she said. Thinking it might be another ploy for attention, James hurried out and purchased a small bottle. Mother claimed some relief, and we left her for the evening.

A GLITCH IN THE PLAN

The next morning, we arrived before seven o'clock in anticipation of the surgery at 7:30. "My throat is still sore," she complained in a hoarse voice.

Nurses came and went, checking Mother's vital signs and giving her pre-op medication. The orderly with a gurney waited outside her room to deliver her to the surgery suite. Suddenly, the door flew open and the surgeon stood over her bed, his hair creeping in a red fringe from under his blue surgical cap.

"Mrs. Ramsey, the nurses tell me you have a fever," he said, placing his stethoscope to her chest. "Yes, I hear a rattle. We'll have to postpone the surgery and get you back to the nursing home. We'll set up a date when your lungs clear."

"Can't I just stay here until I'm better?" Mother asked.

"No, I'm afraid we can't keep people with sore throats and crackly chest sounds," he said with a laugh. And he was gone, leaving us free to return home.

FELLED BY THE FLU

For three weeks, Mother battled a flu virus that filled her lungs with fluid. I worried that the lump in her breast grew while we waited. But, at the moment, the risk of pneumonia from surgery outweighed the danger of the cancer.

While we waited for Mother's improvement, Dad spent his days moving from his bed to his chair to his bedside commode. He refused to eat anything except the grilled cheese sandwiches, which he ordered as if the nurse's station was a fast-food restaurant window.

THE GRIP OF GUILT

On each visit, I walked him in the hallways for exercise, but his conversations were limited to daily fault-finding with the nurses. "They don't care," he said, echoing the list of grievances Mother threw at me when I entered their room. "They won't do anything for you."

Family and friends rallied when I wavered under my growing heap of guilt. "You had no choice in placing your parents in the nursing home. They stayed in their home longer than they should have only because you took care of them," they told me.

But each complaint from Mother and Dad chipped away at my objectivity. Although I visited the home at different time intervals, never seeing the neglect they described, doubt crept into the cracks of my mind, digging out trenches like an enemy in battle. A war raged over what I thought was the best care for my parents and what they wanted—to be in their own home.

What would I have done with Mother while Dad spent a month in the hospital? I questioned myself.

On the other hand, Dad said he never would have needed surgery if the nursing home food had not been rotten. He even blamed the surgeon for his present condition. *And what would I do with him now that I have to be away with Mother in the hospital?* On most days, I wished I had left them in their house, closed the door, and walked away. "But you couldn't have lived with yourself if something even worse had happened to them at home," my husband stated. And I knew he was right.

MORE THAN A STUMBLE

Before one crisis resolved, another cropped up. One evening as my family gathered around the table for spaghetti, the phone interrupted our meal. "Your dad has fallen," a nurse said. "We have the bleeding under control, but I think he may need some stitches."

My daughters and I dropped our forks and rushed to the nursing home. Dad lay on his bed, blood spattered his clothes and a cold compress covered his forehead.

Mother stood over him, wringing her hands. She had been in the dining room and did not know how it happened.

"Going to the bathroom. Hit my head on the door," Dad said in a weak voice.

The nurses found him by the closet, several feet away from the bathroom. But he could answer our questions, so where it happened did not matter.

An ambulance transported Dad to the local hospital. "My, you have a big 'hemo-tomato,'" the ER nurse teased him. He tried a faint smile. The doctor on duty pulled the torn flesh together with a "butterfly," and wrapped his head in gauze. Our family doctor called in orders for Dad to remain in the observation unit overnight. I felt relieved with his decision, knowing that Mother would not rest a minute if she saw him bandaged like a mummy.

A SECOND DATE WITH SURGERY

By the time the nursing staff reported Mother's lungs "clear," only black rings under Dad's eyes and a healing scar on his head reminded us of his mishap with the door. I called the doctor's office to set up a date for surgery, hoping it could be on the Monday following my scheduled conference.But the receptionist reported that he might want to do the surgery on Friday. In case his answer was "Monday," I asked my daughter to drive Mother to the hospital and check her in. James and I could travel from Tulsa to Little Rock on Sunday afternoon and be there almost as early as they were. We packed our trailer and sat by the phone, not knowing whether we would leave for Tulsa or Little Rock. *Lord, You know I need these three days with fellow Christians,* I prayed. *My spirits are sagging. But Mother's well-being is more important. Please send me where I'm supposed to be.*

Whether you turn to the right or to the left, your ears will hear a voice behind you, saying, "This is the way; walk in it."

Isaiah 30:21 (NIV)

Chapter Ten

CANCER AND A CRACKED HIP

At 9:00 on Thursday morning, the phone rang. The nurse from the surgeon's office reported that Mother's surgery was scheduled for Monday morning. She requested that we check her into the hospital on Sunday afternoon.

After a quick call to our daughter, James and I headed for a three-day respite. Everything had fallen into place. We agreed to meet Debbie and Mother on Sunday at the hospital. After checking Mother in, Debbie would return home to sit with Daddy while Mother had the surgery.

Suzanne, another daughter, took charge of our business. I breathed easier while reviewing the plan of action. I believed God had answered my prayer by clearing the way for me to go to Tulsa.

A CHANGE IN THE WIND

But the closer we drove to the Arkansas state line, the darker the sky grew. About an hour from Oklahoma's border, big watery snowflakes plopped against the windshield. "Ten inches of snow has fallen across Arkansas' northern counties," the radio weather forecaster reporter. *This is crazy*, I thought. *Maybe God didn't intend for me to go to this conference.*

White slush formed on the highway, spattering our truck and trailer when we passed another vehicle. The flakes grew larger, hanging like lace doilies on tree limbs and bushes along the roadside. The windshield wipers pushed icy white mounds from side to side. Doubts piling up like snowdrifts along the fence rows filled my head. *Lord, are you telling us that we weren't supposed to go to this conference? After it seemed that you cleared the way, should we turn around?*

While ice wrapped our truck like a warm cocoon, we watched heavy white fluff layer the Oklahoma farmland, changing trees and fence posts into subjects from an enchanted kingdom. The clean snow transformed rusty farm machinery and dirty trash barrels into objects of beauty. Its silent cleansing of the countryside calmed my doubts about my parents' care and the dreaded thoughts of Mother's surgery.

OUT OF THE SNOW AND INTO THE SUN

As we drove onto the turnpike headed northwest, the sky brightened and the white flakes grew smaller. By the time we reached Tulsa in mid-afternoon, the sun had melted all but a trace of snow. *Forgive me, Lord, for doubting your directions and guidance in every aspect of our lives,* I prayed.

James pulled our trailer into a reserved space in the campground dwarfed by concrete and glass high-rises characteristic of a bustling industrial city. Cozy in our home away from home, whizzing traffic on a heavily traveled interstate highway lulled us to sleep.

Like an oasis in the desert, the next day's conference refreshed my depleted mind and body. Old friends and new acquaintances buoyed me with friendliness, fresh ideas, and a new perspective on writing. Little by little, the nagging guilt in leaving Mother and Dad in someone else's care fell away—at least for three days.

THE CALM BEFORE THE STORM

Entering Mother's hospital room on Sunday afternoon, I felt rested and ready to meet head-on the consequences of her surgery. Debbie and her husband had settled Mother into her room. They reported that Dad was doing as well as he had been for the past several months.

On Monday morning, Mother went through the surgery with no apparent problems. The doctor gave an optimistic report on the containment of the cancer. I called Dad at the nursing home to give him the good news. Since his abdominal surgery, his emotions had lingered at skin level, so I was not surprised at his teary-sounding response.

"Grandad is all right," Debbie said, taking the phone. "He's been rather lethargic today. I think he's worried. But I'll assure him again that Grandmother is doing fine."

I stayed at Mother's bedside until early evening. "You can't sit here day and night like you've done before," my husband said, insisting that I hire a private nurse to take charge for a few hours.

I took his advice, believing that Mother was doing exceptionally well following the surgery. *My daughters are looking in on Dad at the nursing home; Mr. Earl is there to cheer him up, and the nurses, despite what Dad thinks, treat him kindly. This crisis will pass. With the coming of spring, their bodies will heal and their spirits will lift.* Hanging onto those thoughts, I drifted into a good sleep.

A DARK CLOUD

The next morning, I answered a knock on my trailer door. A messenger reported that my daughter was on the phone at a neighbor's trailer.

"Mother, I didn't do my job," Debbie's voice came through the line. "Grandad fell this morning. He's broken his hip."

A wave of nausea gripped me. "Oh, no," I cried, unable to take in the details.

"I'm coming with him in the ambulance," she continued. "We'll be at the hospital in about two hours."

What will I tell Mother? Questions raced through my mind. *How will this affect her?*

She had done so well. I decided to break the news to her after her doctor had seen her on morning rounds. But before I could tell her, the emergency unit phoned her room. "Your husband is in the ER," the nurse on duty stated, misunderstanding my orders to call her room, but to give me the message.

Once again, Mother's calmness astounded me. "What are we going to do?" she asked.

"We're going to get his hip fixed, Mother," I said with more confidence than I felt. She lay back against her pillow, seeming to accept my answer.

"Now I have to meet with Dad's doctor. As soon as he's in a room, I'll ask if we can wheel you in a chair to see him." And I hurried off to the emergency room.

A DOUBLE CRISIS

Dad's frail form lay on the gurney, waiting for the surgeon. Pain—hard, unrelenting pain—begged for relief through his strained eyes and clinched teeth. His purple-veined hand clasped Debbie's.

"Just put that pain right here in my hand, Grandad. Let me take it for you," she soothed him. And his knuckles turned white.

For three days, we stood by his bedside, watching helplessly while he suffered. Fluid built up around his heart, preventing the surgery to mend his broken hip. Cardiologists, orthopedic surgeons, and internists kept a constant watch over his progress. My hope that he could make it through a hip-replacement dwindled.

"I've come to stay as long as you need me," Debbie said, unpacking her bag at the trailer. "You have to have some help with both of them hospitalized."

And others came. Dad's sister and Mother's sister. My sister from Texas. We took turns rolling Mother from the third floor to Dad's room on the fifth floor. Together we circled his bed and waited.

The cardiologist finally concluded that Dad's relief from the hip pain took precedence over his unstable heart. His fluid buildup was quite possibly as stable as it would ever get. My aunt sat in the hospital room with Mother during the operation. Once again, my family and I camped out in the surgery waiting room. A needle back and forth pushing across a square of fabric made cross-stitches in a pattern and steadied my hands and thoughts.

Eventually the surgeon announced that Dad had made it through the surgery. He went on to say that the condition of his heart remained "touch and go." Dad was transferred to the intensive care unit.

CARING FOR TWO

Mother continued to improve. No signs of cancer showed up in her lymph nodes and no treatment was ordered. I rejoiced. My sister and I divided our time between Mother's room on one floor and Dad's on another. With Dad so desperately ill, he needed full-time attention, but Mother, for the most part, required entertainment.

After two weeks—longer than Mother's doctor had projected—she was dismissed to her nursing home. My sister had returned to her home in Texas, so I hired a nurse to sit with Dad while I drove her home.

Conversation between us did not come easy. My heart ached for her having to leave Dad once again a hospital in a different town, but my patience strained with her short-attention span for reading or watching television. Once again, the enemy of doubt Mother placed in my head battled my commonsense arrangements for her care.

Over and over from her hospital bed, she had driven home the point of her discontent. "It's not as lovely as you think in the nursing home," she would say. "You believe it's the 'Garden of Eden.'"

"I don't think there are no problems, Mother. But you and Dad can't take care of yourselves at home. You know that," I would reply. Sometimes, I did not respond at all because I had nothing new to say.

From my daily visits to the nursing home and my interaction with the staff, I understood the care did not match an ideal level. Aides, the caregivers with the greatest burden for hands-on care, were understaffed, underpaid, and overworked. Frequent turnovers resulted. Often, the care was inconsistent because the same person did not follow a patient long enough to develop a rapport.

Personal touches were lacking. Some caregivers hurried in tasks of grooming, making Mother and Dad complain of roughness. Baths were scheduled rather than given on a "when-I-feel-like-it basis." Call lights were not answered immediately. Food was institutionally prepared. And long waits to be served in the dining room were one of my parents' most frequent grievances.

I wanted Mother's and Dad's independence to remain intact just as much as they did. I longed for them to have the freedom of eating, dressing, bathing, and napping at their leisure in their own home. But there were no simple solutions to their care.

Physically and emotionally drained from the constant tug-of-war between my head and my heart, I drove my van to the nursing home. I told Mother to remain in her seat while I retrieved a wheelchair.

HOMECOMING

Within a moment, her favorite nurse helped her into the chair. Giving her a hug, she said, "We've missed you, Loree."

She wheeled Mother inside, and other staff members gathered in her room to welcome her home. I felt like a stressed-out mother handing over the care of a toddler to trusted friends.

The nurse knelt beside Mother's chair and took both her hands. "Loree, we have to tell you that Earl died last night," she said.

Mother burst into tears, covering her face with her hands. "What'll we do without him?" she cried. "He was such a good friend."

"Yes, we'll all miss him," the nurse replied. "The staff, one by one, went to the hospital to tell him good-bye."

"I don't want your daddy to know," Mother said, looking up at me.

"He'll have to know, Mother. But I'll tell him when he's stronger."

With that, I gave her a quick hug and left, knowing she was in a safe place. I turned my full attention to Daddy who waited in the hospital an hour's drive away.

Therefore, be clear minded and self-controlled so that you can pray. Above all, love each other deeply because love covers over a multitude of sins. Offer hospitality to one another without grumbling. Each one should use whatever gift he has received to serve others, faithfully administering God's grace in its various forms. If anyone speaks, he should do it as one speaking the very words of God. If anyone serves, he should do it with the strength God provides so that in all things God may be praised through Jesus Christ.

1 Peter 4:7b-10a (NIV)

Chapter Eleven

THE LAST LAP OF DAD'S EARTHLY JOURNEY

"Dear Jesus, take me home," Dad moaned from his hospital bed. I looked up from my notebook, not sure I had understood his words. My eye caught my husband's from behind his newspaper. He nodded. Dad had prayed to die.

For over a week, I had sat by his bedside, leaving only for meals and a few hours of sleep. Daddy refused the food on his tray; he begged to be left alone when the orderlies took him to physical therapy. And he groaned when the nurses turned him from side to side.

When they lifted him into a chair for the prescribed "sitting-up" hour, he cried out in pain. Over and over, he asked: "Why did that doctor do this to me?"

I talked about the beautiful spring flowers blooming outside his window on the hospital campus. I related political news, punch lines from television shows, and funny stories about the family. However, Dad showed no interest in the things we had once discussed.

When I told him about Earl Hostetler's death, his face twisted with emotion. "His heart just wore out," I said.

"I know," Dad answered. "Earl told me when he moved to the home that he had only six months to live."

A COUNSELOR IN A LAB COAT

One morning while he was in physical therapy, I approached the nurse who changed his bed. "Dad is depressed. What do you think about counseling?"

She shook her head. "It takes a long time to see results," she said. "Especially when someone doesn't want help. And in your dad's condition, I'm not sure he'd cooperate. He's not compliant with physical therapy."

Not long after the PT staff returned Dad to his bed, the doctor who had performed his abdominal surgery made a bedside call. He smiled with a greeting, clasping his hand with genuine concern. "Mr. Ramsey," he began. "I've gone back over the records from your stomach surgery and there's no physical reason to prevent you from eating. Why are you refusing your food?"

"I just can't eat it," Daddy answered. "I don't even know why I'm still alive."

"I don't either," the doctor continued. "But if God had intended for you to die, He would have taken you. You've been too close too many times. Obviously, He still has a reason for you to live. Do you believe that?"

Daddy nodded.

"For as long as we're here on this earth, God gives us bodies to live in. But He expects us to feed our bodies. Do understand that, Mr. Ramsey?"

Again, he nodded.

"So I believe God wants you to eat and make that body stronger until He calls you home. Will you do that?"

This time, Daddy spoke. "I'll try."

"Then let's pray that God will help you until He's ready for you," the surgeon continued. He grasped Dad's hand and prayed for his renewed strength.

When the nurse returned, I said, "We don't need a counselor. Dad's doctor was here." And she smiled.

But when the noon meal arrived, Daddy sipped only a small portion of a milkshake. "I can't hold it," he said, waving his shrunken hand over the tray.

Turning away, he again prayed, asking God to let him die.

A DREADED DISMISSAL

After three weeks in the hospital, the orthopedic surgeon transferred Dad to the nursing home. "He refuses to try physical therapy," the doctor said. "We have no reason to keep him here."

I dreaded taking him back to the nursing center, knowing his continuous moans would panic Mother. But I was unprepared for the nurse's report following the first night back together in their room. "The nighttime staff documented that your mother turned on her call light twenty-eight times," she said. "We're moving your dad to a different hall where we have more aides."

The arrangement gave both Mother and Dad—and the nursing staff—some rest. Placed on opposite ends of the building, Mother was forced to exercise, shuffling the length of two halls to visit Dad. Although he lay in resigned silence while she related that she hated living in the nursing home, Dad seemed more at peace.

"As soon as your Daddy's well, we'll move back home," she told me daily.

I explained that Daddy would never be what she termed "well." And certainly, he could never take care of her again in their home. But she turned a deaf ear.

Some mornings, she would circle the nurses' station until she caught the attention of her special nurse. "Arlie is better today. Don't you think?" she would ask.

"Arlie isn't worse, but he's not better," the caring nurse answered, gently prodding Mother to face reality. "In fact, he could die at any time."

But even the nurse's frankness did not pierce the fantasy she spun that they would return home, Dad would take care of her, and they would do the things they did twenty years earlier.

TAKING NOTE OF SMALL THINGS

An aide on Dad's hall took a special interest in him. She noted that he ate better when the breakfast menu included bacon. She suggested that I stash prepared sausage and biscuits, which she could pop in the microwave, in the staff's refrigerator.

At snacktime, Dad refused juice, but agreed to drink root beer. I stocked the refrigerator, and Susie served the cold drink with peanut-butter crackers at mid-morning. Although he still grumbled when the nurses made him sit up for an hour, we made progress in getting more food into his frail body.

LOOKING OUT FOR DAD

One day, I walked down the hallway to Dad's room as Susie rushed out his door. "Your dad refuses to get up," she said. "He says someone dropped him last night. I'm going to report it to the head nurse." Dad lay in his bed, his blue-veined hands gripping the bed rails like a frightened child holding onto a roller coaster. "What's the problem?" I asked. "You know you need to spend some time sitting in your chair."

"They dropped me last night," he said. "And I'm not getting up again."

"Who dropped you?"

"I don't know—you know I can't see to recognize anyone," he went on. "They took me to the bathroom, then dragged me across the floor, and threw me on the bed." His eyes pleaded for me to believe him.

Daddy wore a catheter and depended on a bed pan for bowel movements. There was no reason to take him to the bathroom.

I questioned him again. "They dragged me on my knees, then they laughed, and said they couldn't hold a greased pig. I'm not a pig," he said, his voice choking in tears.

Susie joined me at his bedside. "That's exactly what he told me," she said.

"We believe you, Dad," I said, patting his hand. "It's all right and you don't have to get up today."

I hurried down the hall to the nurses' office. "I don't know what happened that caused the aides to take him to the bathroom," I told her, feeling the tears closing off my throat. "But his feelings are hurt because he thinks someone laughed at him. Daddy doesn't hear well; he might have misunderstood."

"Those are two of our best aides on the evening shift," she said. "They wouldn't get him up to go to the bathroom."

But they did. Although the director of nursing checked into the matter, I never received a satisfactory reason. The aides themselves assured me they did not drag him. They insisted that his legs buckled and they caught him before his knees touched the floor.

I knew the slightest pull on Dad's ravaged body could have felt as though someone threw him on the bed. And I have been in situations where even serious things turned funny. But to an old weakened man who could not see or hear, their laughter rang like ridicule. The explanations did not ease the ache in my heart for Dad's vulnerability. And Mother's and Dad's complaints of unanswered call lights, poor food, and short-tempered nurses returned to haunt me.

In retrospect, I wish I had pursued the incident with greater indignation. Whether intentional or not, I believe Dad's treatment was inappropriate. And I think the aides were defended by the director of nursing when she knew they had handled a patient with a lack of compassion.

On the other hand, I understand the position family members are in when their loved ones live in a nursing facility. At that point, the deed was done. If I had responded in anger, I doubt that anything would have changed, except my rapport with the staff.

For some months, one aide responsible for Dad's discomfort and humiliation skirted me in the hallways. But later on, she became someone I could depend on for Mother's care. I believe family members should pay attention to details and incidents in the nursing home. But I recognize the situation of long-term care is imperfect and as caregivers, we are responsible only to do our best for our loved ones.

LOSS OF DIGNITY

One afternoon following the unfortunate situation, I pushed Dad's door ajar to see several nurses around his bed. One held a Polaroid camera and was clicking pictures of his exposed backside. Dad lay on one side, his face a mask of resignation.

The nurse in charge explained they had to document the condition of his skin breakdown following a hospital stay. I understood the policy of an institution and the reasons they cover themselves against charges of negligence. But my heart wrenched at Dad's loss of dignity.

In all my growing-up years, he was the person in our household who went to the bathroom, pulled the curtains tight, and covered the keyhole. I never heard him name a private body part, much less speak of its functions. But during the past year, I had watched my modest, sensitive Dad reduce himself to a survivor's mentality.

Have I done this by placing him in a nursing home's care? I questioned. *Or has the pain and trauma of three major surgeries within a year, leaving him with a worn-out body, robbed him of his fight?*

INSIGHT FROM SILENCE

On most of my daily visits to the nursing home, Mother joined me at Dad's bedside. I noticed that he grew quiet, often closing his eyes while I recounted tidbits of news from church, family, and friends. At 5:00, Mother left for the dining room while I waited to help Daddy with his supper tray. That hour became our time to talk.

One day as Mother's shadow passed the doorway, Daddy said: "Your mother thinks she has lots of problems living here. I would love to go home, too, but I know it's not possible."

Thinking over the phone conversation I had had with Mother that morning, I picked up a broader insight into Daddy's words. "Your dad won't talk to me so I'm not going back to visit him again," she had called to tell me. "I might as well move back home. I only came to take care of him, but he doesn't need me here."

Daddy can't fight Mother's battles anymore, I suddenly realized. *He's coping by withdrawing from her. How sad for both of them.*

Like a giant puzzle, the pieces of my parents' life began to fit together. Dad had spent fifty-six years meeting Mother's every need, making sure not one of her requests was denied. He was the buffer between her and the real world. Now the one thing she wanted —to live in her own house and have him take care of her again —he could not give. So like shades on the windows of his soul, he closed his eyes and lips and shut her out.

I'm so sorry, Daddy, I wanted to say. *Sorry for you and sorry for Mother.* But they had drawn the pattern for their lifestyle themselves. It was not my fault their lives had ended in ill health within the confines of a nursing home. Not my fault, but my responsibility. Without saying a word, I knew Daddy had handed the reins to me. He was too tired to cope any longer.

"Would you like me to read from the Bible?" I asked, bringing myself back to the present.

"Yes," he answered.

I opened a small booklet I had left on Dad's table for our suppertime devotions. "God's Promises" the cover proclaimed. I opened to the verse, *You can get anything —anything you ask for in prayer—if you believe,* from Matthew 21:22 (TLB)

Dad and I both knew the prayer of his heart. I had heard him ask aloud for weeks: "God take this tired body out of its pain. Take me home with You."

As I read that promise, I looked at Dad's diminishing body lying helpless under the bedcovers. His weaken legs and humped back no longer supported his weight for simple daily functions. His clouded eyes saw only bulky forms against the light; his ears interpreted fragments of sentences and laughter as mockery. He knew Sunday from Thursday and morning from night only when someone bent close to speak in his ear.

God, this is no life. I'm ready, too, for him to go home. And I released Daddy to God's will. The next afternoon, he was gone.

Let us hold unswervingly to the hope we profess, for He who promised is faithful.

HEBREWS 10:23 (NIV)

Chapter Twelve

GOOD-BYE, DAD

Brown grocery sacks lined the kitchen counters. With one hand in fresh hamburger meat, rounding out patties for the freezer, I reached with the other to grab the wall phone on its first ring.

"We're losing Mr. Ramsey," the nurse's voice came through the receiver.

I shoved the meat and fresh vegetables into the refrigerator and took time to dial my daughter's office. "Grandad's dying," I said before running for the door. Breaking speed limits, I raced across town to the nursing home.

When I entered the lobby, nurses rolled Dad from the whirlpool bath to his room. One look at his ashen face and I knew he was already gone. Family gathered with me in the hallway outside his door.

"Where's your mother?" they asked.

"She's taking a nap," I answered, thankful they no longer shared a room. Standing by while the staff worked over Daddy would have been devastating for Mother.

Dad's special aide came from his room. "I told him you're here and he smiled," she said, squeezing my hand. But I knew in my heart that Dad was no longer trapped in his dysfunctional body.

Another nurse brushed by. "No heroic measures," I told her. "Let him go."

In a few moments, the nurse opened the door and asked us to go in. "Good-bye, Dad," I said, kissing his forehead as I'd done the evening before.

"He was such a good Daddy," I told the others, tears streaming down my face.

A kaleidoscope of pictures filtered through my mind. Daddy running with strong legs that once walked behind a plow; Daddy looking down on us with sharp eyes that had tracked rabbits; Daddy listening with keen ears that had heard birds chirping and wind howling around his childhood home.

I could not be sad. He was free. My tears fell for the talks I would miss; the Christian faith we shared. It's what the Bible calls "like-mindedness."

NO TIME TO REFLECT

My thoughts turned to Mother, bound to a life she hated and would now have to face without him. The staff accompanied my family and me to her room. I cracked the door and watched her peaceful sleep. With all my heart, I wished I could spare her this grief.

"Mother," I said, gently shaking her awake. "Daddy's gone. It's just happened."

"No, no, no," she screamed, covering her face with her hands. "It can't be. I was just there this morning. We had a snack together."

Unable to console her, I stepped aside while my daughters and aunts smothered her with hugs and words of comfort.

"I have to go home," she said, drawing herself up straight. "There's no reason for me to stay here now."

Kneeling beside her, I said, "Mother, we can't open your house. Remember, there's no water, no gas, no airconditioning.

"I'll take you to my home where we'll all be together. But you have to promise me you'll come back here this evening."

Family members shot me an astonished look. "Can't she stay for a few days at your home?"

"No," I answered. I knew Mother well. If she stayed away for even one night, she would never return to the nursing home.

"I'll stay here with you tonight, but you have to promise me you'll come back. The nurses have your medication and you'll rest better in your familiar bed."

Reluctantly, she agreed. We helped her dress to receive the guests who would be calling to offer condolences.

MY HEAD OVERRULING MY HEART

That evening, I slept in a chair by Mother's bed. The nurses came and went, offering her kind words of comfort. In a few hours, she drifted off to sleep.

The next morning, her sister arrived to help her dress. I slipped out to ready my home for the family and friends filling every corner. Funeral arrangements, meal preparations, and hanging tough with Mother pushed grief to the back of my mind.

Understanding that Mother needed time to say good-bye to Dad, we spent several hours at the funeral home. I overheard her telling friends, "I'm going home now."

"You know you can't stay there alone," they would answer. But she insisted.

By evening, Mother had made her own arrangements for a widowed cousin to sleep with her at the nursing home. "I can't spend the night before your Daddy is buried alone," she said.

"But you are not alone," I countered. "That's why you live in the nursing home. Someone is always there to check on you."

"They're not family. They don't care," she responded.

"I don't even know if they'll let someone come in to stay with you. I'll have to ask."

The nurse on duty listened to my explanation that Mother did not want to sleep in her room alone. "We can make an exception tonight," she said. "But not on a long-term basis."

I assured her this would be the only night. Again, family members questioned me. "What would it hurt for her to stay here for a few nights?"

"This won't be any easier to face three nights from now than it is tonight," I said, knowing I had made an unpopular decision. I talked a tough game, but inside the guilt trap opened wider and swallowed up the nagging unease that drained me. I hated being firm with Mother when I knew her heart was breaking.

But, I looked beyond the funeral. There were rough days ahead—days when everyone else would go back to their homes and I would be left alone to fight my battles. Yet, looking back, I still second-guess my rigid viewpoint.

LINGERING REGRETS

A friend once told me that a daughter's brain is comparable to a tape player. All incidents and annoyances are stored, and a word or act from a mother triggers a response to circumstances from the past. Despite the traumatic loss of Dad in Mother's life, her insistence in having a family member with her dredged up old patterns of her irrational dependence on others for daily decisions and socialization. I wonder if my irritation and frustration dulled my compassion. I worry that I was not understanding of Mother's deep loss—that I did not express to her an extra measure of love.

THE DAY AT HAND

My sister and her family arrived only an hour before the funeral service. We stood with Mother by Daddy's casket, saying our final good-byes. "Your Daddy's the only man I ever loved," she said through her tears.

I looked at my own husband. I could only imagine what she felt in giving up a life-long companion. I would miss Daddy, but it was not the same as giving up the mate who slept beside you, shared your memories, and held you up when you stumbled.

We scheduled the service for mid-morning, before the late June heat could sap Mother's stamina. Our pastor, at my request, read the scripture I had read to Dad the night before he died. *You can get anything you ask for in prayer . . . if you believe*, from Matthew 21:22. I knew Dad had received the prayer of his heart.

The pastor comforted us by admitting his own heart was heavy. "But knowing that Jesus reigns as King of Kings and Lord of Lords, our heartaches begin to fade," he said. "He reigns over sickness that attempts to intimidate us."

Remembering the three major surgeries Dad had endured during the past year, I knew too well how sickness had intimidated him. He had lost his sense of humor, his modesty, and his will to live. But he never gave up on Jesus taking him home.

"Jesus reigns over sorrow that could drown us and over death that would destroy us," I heard our pastor continue.

There had been times, looking at Dad's body, helpless and bombarded with pain, that I wondered if we were all drowning.

From Romans 8:37, the preacher continued, "No, in all these things we are more than conquerors through Him who loved us." Right there in the midst of sorrow, joy joined with peace in my heart. Through his belief in Jesus Christ, I knew Daddy had conquered death.

The pastor closed the service with Jeremiah 29:11. I hoped Mother could grasp the words " . . . I give you a future and a hope."

LIFE GOES ON . . .

In the weeks that followed Daddy's death, we tried to ease Mother's adjustment with boat rides, picnics, and family dinners. Although she conceded to stay at the nursing home for a while, she channeled her energy into moving to her house rather than making a home at the facility. My heart bled for her double loss—Daddy and her home. But there was no practical solution for keeping Mother anywhere except in the nursing center.

MOTHER'S CAMPAIGN

One day in the nursing-home lobby, she announced: "I have to go home." A young paraplegic resident who had no choices about his residence spoke up: "Mrs. Ramsey, you are at home."

Her eyes flashed and her voice cut the air. "This will never be my home."

Trying to not upset her with Dad's death still so fresh in our hearts, I ignored her strategies to manipulate me. I had explained over and over the reasons for her residence in the nursing home. Each time we ended in an argument.

One day, she phoned. "Couldn't we just talk about this?" she asked.

"Yes, we can talk about it, Mother. But nothing is going to change. You can't—and won't—live by yourself. I can't find anyone to live with you. If I did, we couldn't afford to pay for around-the-clock live-in services.

"We've been over the same thing day in and day out. Your health requires that you have medication regularly. And you didn't take it properly when you lived at home with Daddy. So what would be different now?"

"I thought we could discuss this reasonably," she countered.

If I had not been so frustrated, I might have laughed. "You think I'm unreasonable because I don't agree with you," I responded.

But my patience wore thin. "Mother, your needs are met. If I fell dead today, I would know that you have proper care. That's a consolation to me.

"But if you can figure out something different, then you do it. I'm not making any other arrangements."

Her argument typically ended with an air of resignation spoken to appeal to my guilt: "I'm not going to live long anyway."

MORE DESPERATE PLEAS

When Mother's prediction of her imminent death failed to get my attention, she told her older sister she would kill herself if she could get her hands on poison. At first, I did not take it seriously, but the threats continued. She mentioned suicide, not only to my aunt, but also to my son, Tim.

One day in desperation, she sent a blood-curdling scream into my ear on the other end of the telephone. Mother's guilt trap opened wider and held me fast.

I considered moving her out of the nursing home, but I had experienced taking care of her at home. I knew I could not cope with her demands for an extended time. At least at the nursing home, I had the buffer of a nursing staff between us. I knew her medications were monitored. And when she insisted that some part of her body was sick or broken, I had the opinion of a professional to help me sort out her needs.

On the other hand, I could not walk away because I was not sure if she sought attention through her threats or if something was actually wrong. Mother's hurts turned my emotions upside-down. Sometimes my anger overrode my compassion. Other times, I watched her scoot her feet down the nursing home corridor, and my heart dragged behind her heels.

SEEKING ANSWERS

God's strength is perfected in our weakest moments, I read in my daily devotional. Mother had certainly experienced the weakest points of life without Dad at her side. And propelled by years of his training, I had tried to take up his task in satisfying her needs.

Mother is eighty years old, I said to myself. *She'll never change. But in smoothing out the rough spots for her, did I usurp God's power to work in her life?*

As a little girl, I remember watching Mother gently peel away a piece of eggshell so a tiny chick could peck its way into the world. That egg had to be broken before new life could emerge. Mother could have removed the entire shell, but she must have understood God's plan for the baby chicken to strengthen itself by struggling from its dark enclosure into bright daylight.

Intuitively, I knew I had to separate God's will for my future from His plan for Mother's life. Although Mother and I are each God's daughters, He has unique plans for us. That realization prompted yet another collision between our heads and our hearts.

In moments of logical thinking, I acknowledged that if I continued to allow Mother's depression, self-pity, and sad circumstances to dominate my thoughts, I would not be physically or mentally able to minister to my husband, my children, or even to her. Sorting things out with my head rather than my heart, I knew I had to do all I could to meet her needs. After that, I had to commit myself to accomplishing whatever God had in store for me. But the emotionally charged cord that mysteriously binds a daughter to her mother encircles the heart and threatens the breath of objectivity. Only God's love can empower relationships with the freedom and confidence for parents and children to respect each other's uniqueness while supporting one another physically, emotionally, and spiritually.

And I am sure that God who began the good work within you will keep right on helping you grow in His grace until His task within you is finally finished on that day when Jesus Christ returns.

PHILIPPIANS 1:6 (TLB)

Chapter Thirteen

TURNING OVER A NEW LEAF

Growing up, I remember times when I would misbehave. After Mother punished me, she would soothe my tears and say, "We're turning over a new leaf."

At first, I imagined actually going out to the trees and turning over green leaves. As I grew older, I pictured a giant-sized book for recording children's good and bad deeds. Slowly, my mother would turn over a clean page—one that did not have my naughty acts numbered in a long list. The crisp, white paper gave me another chance to draw in happy pictures and secure feelings.

Now it was Mother's time to turn over a new leaf. After a few weeks of adjustment following Dad's death, the nursing home staff paraded roommates in and out of her quarters, trying to find someone compatible. Like a queen reigning from a throne, Mother sat in her recliner, interviewing each one and setting the house rules. If they stepped beyond a guest status, she demanded that they move out.

HARMONY FOR A SPELL

Then came Agnes, a meek, small-framed woman with work-worn hands. Mother enjoyed her company, but I noticed that she followed Mother's lead like a puppy obeying its mistress. Agnes watched television, tuned to whatever program Mother chose. She talked when Mother listened and fell asleep in her chair when Mother napped.

The Christmas season approached, and Mother delayed her moving home day until spring. But like a glass-tree ornament crashing to the floor, the administrator burst my reprieve. As I entered the nursing home for the Christmas party, he called me into his office.

"Agnes is moving after the holidays," he said. "Her children are taking her to a home closer to them."

"This can't be happening," I answered. "Just when Mother found someone she likes."

"The staff and I believe your mother is too possessive of that room," he continued. "We think she looks on it as 'hers and her husband's,' and anyone else is merely a guest, subject to her approval. Moving her to another room might help her face reality."

I conceded that Mother wanted her own way, but I could not accept that it had anything to do with the room.

"You may be right," the administrator said. "But I've seen new surroundings make a difference in other cases. I wanted you to know that if she continues rejecting roommates, we need to change her location."

At least, we'll get through Christmas before Agnes leaves, I thought, returning to the festive music of the party.

AFTER AGNES

Beginning in January, other ladies moved into Mother's room. One was a little deaf woman named Mary who had no family.

"A good match," the director of nursing said. "She has no personal belongings, so your mother's furnishings can remain intact. And she uses her room mainly for sleeping. It will be almost as though your mother has no roommate.

But Mother did not view Mary with the same objectivity. "She's crazy," she insisted. "I won't have her in my room. This morning, she put on my blouse."

I picked up on the possessive words. Maybe the administrator is right. Then Mother's tears swayed me. *It can't be the room, I argued with myself. If we could just find someone like Agnes. . . .*

NEXT IN LINE

The staff moved Mary and another lady took her place. Mother met me in the lobby. "I'm afraid of her," she said. "She accused me of tying her up. I never touched her!"

I knocked on the nurse's office door. "Mother is afraid of this woman. Do you plan to move her?" I asked.

"Yes," she answered. "Later this afternoon, but the woman isn't dangerous. She's had a stroke and is going through nicotine withdrawal." I sensed her impatience.

"I told your mother the next time someone moves, it has to be her," she went on. I nodded in agreement. The staff had gone extra lengths to satisfy Mother. I could not challenge their position.

THE SHOWDOWN

The next afternoon, Mother phoned in a hysterical state. "You have to come right now! They said I have to move. This is my room and I'm not leaving."

One of Mother's friends had dropped by for a visit. She took the receiver. "Your mother is all right, and you don't need to come," she said. "There's been some misunderstanding about her asking the new roommate to leave."

The friend assured me that she would stay with Mother for a while. I ended our conversation and dialed the director of nursing. She explained that a woman recovering from a stroke had been transferred from the hospital. She had asked for a small fan to blow on her while in bed and that triggered Mother's disapproval. Within half an hour, she had ordered the lady out of the room. Her daughters had requested that their mother be moved to another room.

"Although I issued your mother an ultimatum and she knows that I don't back down, I have one other lady who has agreed to room with her," the nurse continued. The woman she named had wanted for some time to share Mother's room, but Mother considered her to be coarse and had refused.

Now, it seemed, she had no choice. I thanked the nurse for extending her one last chance to remain in the room of her choice. And I agreed to meet with the staff to review her care plan on the following day.

WORDS OF ENCOURAGEMENT

Later that evening, Mother's friend phoned. "I had no idea how miserable your mother is," she said. "All she talked about is going home. I told her that if there was any way she could live in her home alone, her family would have already moved her.

"I wish there was more I could say or do to change her attitude," she continued. "But let me assure you that one day you'll forget all these unpleasant situations with your parents. You'll remember only the good times."

I thanked her for the encouragement, but I wondered, *Would I ever recall happy times?* For the past five years, the care of my parents had taken on a life of its own. My husband, my children, the writing career I had planned—even my own well-being—stood neglected while I played tug-of-war over what I thought was best for Mother and Dad and what they wanted to do. All I wished for was their happiness and safety. Why could they not understand?

MEETING THE STAFF

Mother's constant complaints planted doubts in my mind about her appropriate care. Questions clicked in my head as I met the staff to discuss her care. I carried a list of her daily grievances: no one answered the call light, the food was burned—or raw. Her clothes did not return from the laundry, her bedclothes were soaked from "night sweats."

But the nurses met me head-on with their list. They named roommates that I did not know about. Some had stayed only one night before moving to another room. One little lady had pulled her chair into the hallway and refused to budge until they settled her into a different room. Still another had requested at the office that she not be asked to share living quarters with Mother.

I listened, stunned by their documentation, yet knowing that everything they outlined would be logical in Mother's way of thinking. Even living in her own home, she had never been a person to leave well-enough alone. "Busy-bodying," I had called it when she complained that her neighbors had too many cars parked in their driveway.

Her lack of patience was classic. One Saturday when she could still walk to her sister's home across the street from hers, she noticed a stray cat had been killed by a passing car. Putting their heads together, she and my aunt decided something had to be done—immediately. Mother phoned the police station to request that the dogcatcher remove the cat's carcass.

The dispatcher stated that no one was on duty on weekends, but he offered to report it first thing Monday morning. Not to be outdone, Mother dialed the mayor, who was my son-in-law's father. I did not know until two years later that he personally removed the dead cat that Saturday afternoon.

For years, I had experienced the lengths Mother went to get her own way. Yet, how could I believe what they said when her version was so different?

"What about the roommate who accused Mother of tying her up?" I asked.

"The lady untied her restraints," one nurse said. "And an aide saw your mother at her bedside trying to retie them."

I could picture Mother doing that. In her mind, she called it "helping." And in the woman's state of mind, Mother was trespassing her rights.

"What about the wet gowns?" I questioned. "I'm worried that she'll fall trying to dress herself in the middle of the night."

"She doesn't ring for help and the next morning, we find no evidence of soaked nightgowns," the nurse answered. "The kind of 'night sweats' she describes are frightening. I know your mother too well. If she experienced one like that, she'd be calling for help."

I thought about one of my friends taking medication for cancer therapy. She often changed her gowns five times in a single night. I knew Mother, too. She would have panicked if she had gone through that experience.

LOOKING AT THE BIG PICTURE

Slowly, I came face-to-face with Mother's manipulation. She used me as yet another vehicle to get her own way. When she complained to me, I complained to the staff. When she threatened me with everything from nervous breakdowns to suicide, I frantically sought solutions.

"Your mother will never be happy," one nurse in the meeting spoke up. "No matter what you do or how much you do—even if you moved her back to her home—she won't be happy."

I had said almost those exact words to Mother, remembering the days in her home when she refused to stir from her recliner as she repeated, "I'm going to die if something isn't done!"

Mother was not happy then even with Daddy hovering over her, rubbing her back, fetching glasses of juice, and acting as the mediator for her demands to see the doctor.

"There's one other thing to cover," the director of nursing spoke through my thoughts. "We don't believe your mother is suicidal. But she has made threats, and we can't guarantee that she can't do something to harm herself even with our safety precautions.

"I've seen a patient drink water from a mop bucket before we could get to him," she continued. "We think your mother is desperately trying to get your attention, but nevertheless, I've scheduled a psychological evaluation."

The neurologist who diagnosed Mother's Parkinson's had suggested psychological help. An anxious woman, he called her. But I didn't believe she would respond. *What if I had followed through? What if? What if?*

If any of you lacks wisdom, he should ask God, who gives generously to all without finding fault, and it will be given to him. But when he asks, he must believe and not doubt, because he who doubts is like a wave of the sea, blown and tossed by the wind.

JAMES 1:5–6 (NIV)

CHAPTER FOURTEEN

WHO NEEDS HELP?

The staff offered to transport Mother to her appointment at the mental health clinic, but I agreed to drive her. We sat in the waiting room for half an hour.

"I'm not crazy," Mother said, fidgeting in her chair. "I don't need to be here."

"No one thinks you're crazy, Mother," I assured her, the knot in my stomach twisting tighter.

"You wouldn't like to live in the nursing home either," she went on.

"I know, but I probably will live there one day," I answered with the same pat words I had used over and over for months.

"No, you won't," she said. "You're young."

The psychologist appeared in the doorway. To my surprise, she invited me into the session.

Mother sat across from her and smiled sweetly while she answered questions. "Everything was wonderful until my husband died," she said. "We lived in our home, enjoyed each other and our children. They came all the time and we had dinners together—good times."

I clinched my fists in my lap. I could not remember when we last had a dinner at Mother's. *How can she believe everything was wonderful before Daddy died? The past year with them in the nursing home together was one long battle of wills. And before in their home, nothing pleased her—not even Daddy.*

Suddenly, the therapist whirled her chair to face me. "Are you angry?" she asked.

"No, I'm fine," I lied, thinking any moment I might explode into tiny pieces and splatter her carpeted floor.

She turned again to Mother. "You are in the grieving process," she said. And she outlined the normal stages of grief. Mother nodded.

"Are you ever angry with anyone?" she asked.

"My goodness, no," Mother replied with a laugh. "I like everyone."

I could hold my emotions no longer. "Mother, you'd better think that over," I said in a controlled voice. "What about the times you scream at me over the telephone? What about your roommate? The nurses?"

"Well, I don't like my roommate," she said.

"What don't you like about her?" the therapist asked.

"She smells and she's bossy."

"And what about saying you were going to kill yourself?"

"I didn't mean that," Mother replied. "I was upset and I just said it. I'd never do anything like that because I think it's a sin."

"Do you think it's wrong to lie?"

"Yes, it's a sin to lie."

"Then, Mrs. Ramsey, when you told your daughter, your grandson, and your sister that you were going to kill yourself, and you didn't mean to do it, you lied."

"I don't know why I said it," she continued. "I'd never take my life. I don't know why my daughter told the nurses."

"Because she cares about you and they care about you. Threatening to kill yourself is not casual conversation. They have to pay attention."

And the therapist turned to me again. "Are you all right?"

"Yes," I answered.

The session ended with the therapist's words: "Mrs. Ramsey, I don't think you are suicidal. But you must remember that what you say affects other people. I'm going to report your case to our staff psychiatrist, but I don't think he'll recommend that you have another visit."

She walked us to the lobby. Touching my arm, she said, "If you need me, call."

In stunned silence, I drove Mother back to the nursing home. I could not believe the masquerade she had just staged. *Mother lives in a world of make-believe. She really thinks her life is as she portrayed. Or does she? Is this a front to manipulate me? How can I even think that my own mother would maneuver situations to get her own way?*

The questions stung. *I need help to sort this out,* I thought.

After I walked Mother back to her room and reported to the nurse, I drove straight home and called the psychologist.

We are pressed on every side by troubles, but not crushed and broken. We are perplexed because we don't know why things happen as they do, but we don't give up and quit.

II CORINTHIANS 4:8 (TLB)

Chapter Fifteen

IT'S OKAY TO SAY NO

For all practical matters, our mother-daughter roles had reversed. I took on the mother's responsibility for physical and financial care. Mother became the child, depending on me to pay her bills, make her decisions, drive her to the beauty shop, and mend her hurts. But Mother would always be Mother. There could never be a complete switch.

It was difficult to be objective because Mother's words had always been absolute to me. I had to become a middle-aged woman to look backward and recognize that she and I had different viewpoints—and it was okay to say no.

AN EXCEPTION TO MOTHER'S RULE

I remember a four-year-old's birthday party. Mother dressed me up in pink organdy ruffles and white patent leather shoes before driving me to the birthday girl's home. "Don't leave for any reason. I'll come back to pick you up," she said.

Halfway through the party, my friend's mother announced: "Boys and girls, we're going downtown to the restaurant for ice cream and birthday cake."

She lined up the preschoolers and headed for her station wagon. But I refused to budge. My mother had said I could not leave and that meant I could not leave.

The other mother tried persuasion, bribery, and threats of a spanking. Still, I would not get into her car. She finally overpowered my kicking legs and screaming lungs and stuffed me into the backseat. I sat sobbing while the others licked ice cream cones and squealed when the honoree blew out four candles on a decorated cake.

When Mother picked me up, the other child's mother told her how I had almost ruined the party with my tantrum. And Mother, embarrassed at my behavior, took her side. Two full-sized women stood over me, arms folded, and eyes glaring. I had obeyed, but no one understood.

WHEN IS ENOUGH ENOUGH?

The same feeling returned when I sat down in the plush armchair next to the psychologist's desk. I pored out my battered emotions, hoping she would help me regain a balance in my life. At the same time, I resented the time the sessions took away from my writing schedule and the money the charges cut from my personal budget.

It's not fair, I grumbled to myself. *I'm here because of Mother's problems—responsibilities I never wanted in the first place!*

But the therapist slammed her hand on the desk. "Enough is enough," she said. "You don't owe your parents your life. You've arranged for your mother to live in a warm or cool, dry, safe, and clean environment. Her food is prepared and her medicine is given properly. When she's ill, the staff consults the doctor. The financial arrangement is manageable.

"What more can you do?" she asked.

I nodded, feeling a weight lift when she explained my situation from that perspective. Teetering on a fresh insight, I thought, *maybe I have done my best.*

But what about Mother's house, its darkened windows and dirt encrusted porches reminding me each time I passed that the one longing of her heart could not be fulfilled?

My husband, my sister, even my children, encouraged me to dispose of the property. I knew all the reasons why it should be sold: danger of theft, general deterioration, possible loss of insurance, money for Mother's care. The psychologist supported my family.

"The house is the tangible issue you and your mother fight over," she said. "The real problem is facing her down in a decision."

She looked at me with steady eyes. "Sell the house," her authoritative voice said.

THE HOUSE ISSUE

The following Sunday, my husband and I took Mother to a restaurant for lunch. Steaming plates of food were set before us. Conversation bounced back and forth in pleasant tones.

Suddenly out of nowhere, James leaned over the table and spoke to Mother. "Why don't you take a tablet and pen and begin listing some of the things in your house that you'd like for your daughters and grandchildren to have?"

A bomb might as well have dropped in the center of the table. "I don't intend for anyone to have anything in my house," she said.

"But the house needs to be sold," James countered. "It's deteriorating day by day. Looks to me like you'd rather decide for yourself what you want each one to have."

"I'm going to live in my house," she exclaimed, getting louder with each response.

I scooted green beans around my plate and watched friends at the next table smile knowingly. "You can't ever live in that house again," my husband said in a controlled, yet strong voice. "In the first place, it would cost too much to repair it and get everything in running order after being shut down for two years.

And that's not considering the fact that you can't live alone."

"I'd rather burn it down!" Mother answered.

My husband looked at me. "I have an appointment," he said, folding his napkin. "I'll walk the few blocks home and get my truck. You can drive your Mother back to the home."

Thanks, I thought. *Stir all this up, then leave me.* As he passed my chair, I considered tripping him.

After that scene, chocolate pie tasted like a brown cardboard box. I managed to walk Mother back to my van. All the way across town to the nursing home, she continued her argument to move home.

"Mother, everything James said is right. I've told you the same things before," I said. "It doesn't make sense for the house to set empty when you can't live in it. But I'm not going to sell it right now. That doesn't mean we won't have to later because you will eventually need the money for your living expenses."

"I just never thought my life would end up like this," she said. Mother closed all our conversations with one of two sentences, pouring out guilt that seeped into the crevices of my inner being. "I hope God calls me home soon . . . maybe tonight," she continued.

For months, I had countered her statements with logical answers such as, "You won't die until God is ready for you to die."

Once I even questioned: "Didn't you and Daddy ever think about what you were going to do in your old age? Didn't you ever make any plans for this stage of your life?"

"No," she answered. "I thought we had our savings and we'd always live in our house." She stopped short of saying, ". . . and Daddy would take care of me."

IT'S TOUGH FOR DAUGHTERS TO TELL MOTHERS NO!

My mind ran out of arguments. I had said the same thing over and over and Mother refused to listen. To maintain some sort of sanity, I distanced myself by saying: "If you can figure out who will stay with you and who will pay all the bills, then you can go home."

The nursing staff and my therapist pointed out that I gave her false hope. Mother interpreted any statement into whatever suited her best. She even told the nurses that I had said she could go home.

"When she says she is moving home, you must confront her, saying that she cannot physically manage a lifestyle alone," they advised. "You must help her face reality."

I longed to replace Mother's dark and gloomy viewpoint with a bright and shiny faith. But I did not know how. Our wills crossed in a deadlock. My everyday routines that wove contentment into the fabric of life were overshadowed by her unhappiness. Simples tasks such as preparing supper or shopping for groceries reminded me that Mother no longer had a home to clean or decorate. She could not choose her own meals, much less prepare them.

Constantly in my thoughts were questions: *Is Mother having anything she likes to eat tonight? Strange hands are helping her bathe and dress. Are they touching her with kindness?*

A REALITY CHECK

Something had to change. I recognized cracks in my own health—a knotted stomach, stiff neck, and constant fatigue. Mentally, I felt out of control.

Three minor car accidents within two weeks confirmed the warnings of my family that I might crumble under the stress. Somehow, Mother and I had to strike a happy medium in our war of wills.

Following the psychologist's advice, I responded to her plans to move home with a definite "no." I set limits on her demands to drive her to visit her sister several afternoons a week. Learning to put my own needs to write, clean my house, or run personal errands ahead of Mother's requests forced me to take a tough stand. She pulled out all the stops to make me feel guilty, including a renewed strategy to replace her roommate.

Although the director of nursing had given an ultimatum when the eighth roommate moved in, Mother set about to relocate the lady. One day the nurse called. "I had found another room for the woman who lives with your mother," she said. "But Mrs. Ramsey told the other women on her hall that she is unpleasant to live with. Now no one will accept her as a roommate. I have no choice. Your mother has to move to another room."

A STRUGGLE AGAINST CHANGE

I agreed that the director had gone beyond her duty to please Mother. The formal notification in writing that the change would take place within ten days arrived in Mother's room. "I won't move," she said waving the letter in my face. "This is my room and I won't move!"

On the appointed day, the nursing director phoned again. "We're moving your mother after lunch today."

"Do you want me to come?"

"I think it would be better if you didn't. I'll call again if I need you."

Shortly after noon, Mother called. "Come right now," she screamed into the phone. "I need help."

"We've told you over and over this was going to happen. It's out of my hands now," I replied with more objectivity than I felt. "I'll be up to see you later, but I'm not coming now."

Within an hour, the nurse called to say that Mother was transferred to her new space. "It was an ugly scene," she said. "We packed her things while she tried everything from hysterics to sweetness to keep us from changing her room. Her ultimate plea was, "I'm a member of the First Baptist Church. You can't do this to me!"

My heart broke that Mother had been reduced to such childish tactics. But for my own sanity, I knew I had to keep a healthy distance from the problem. I recalled that in the event of an emergency on airlines the personnel advises persons caring for a child to put their own oxygen mask in place first. An adult cannot care for a child without caring for herself first.

While my instincts were to place Mother's needs first at all costs, I recognized that I could not care for her at all if I depleted my physical and emotional reserves. I had to learn a tough lesson in that I could not be all things to Mother. I had to step back and allow her to fight some of her own battles.

OTHER HELPING HANDS

The day of the move, the assistant nursing director pushed Mother's wheelchair to her new room. A special friend and one who had reached out to Mother with kindness, I was thankful she was on duty.

Many had touched Mother with love and kindness—the nursing home staff, our pastor and church family, a host of friends. Mother had suffered losses starting with her health and ending with her husband and ultimately, her home. Yet, she still had so much to live for; so much to share with others. I prayed God would help her to understand His plan for her future.

Later that evening, my husband and I visited Mother in her new bedroom. While I felt physically drained just from knowing about the ordeal of the day, Mother showed little trace of her earlier hysterical state. I watched her arrange belongings in a bureau drawer and thought about my emotional afternoon, working at my desk but thinking about her being forced to move to a different room. Despite knowing that she had contributed to the situation by being uncooperative, my heart was still heavy.

A DOSE OF HER OWN MEDICINE

The next morning, the nursing director reported again. Mother had waited at the front door for her.

"I can't stay in that room," she told the nurse. "The lady living there said she didn't want me."

The nurse said she patted Mother's and hand replied, "Now you know how your roommates felt."

"Oh, no. I never said anything like that to them," Mother argued.

"But you did," the director told her. "And their feelings were hurt just like yours are now."

A SLIGHT TURNAROUND

The move turned Mother's direction. A small turn, but nevertheless, a positive step. She began to make herself at home and admitted she liked the new living space as well as the other one.

"You were right," I said to the administrator, acknowledging that Mother had been too possessive about the room she had shared with Daddy.

"Although I'm trained in these matters, I don't always have the answers," he said. "But sometimes, as in your mother's case, we have to try all alternatives."

Despite her acceptance of the new room, Mother picked up her dogged determination to move into her own home. I prepared her for the inevitable, stating at every opportunity that the house needed to go on the market. But my will turned to jelly at the thought of actually going against her. *Why should I put myself through the mental anguish of battling over this issue?* I reasoned. *I can't do it now.*

SEEKING MY OWN PEACE

I ended my sessions with the psychologist, feeling stronger and more secure. The weeks of counseling had brought to the surface my acceptance that Mother might never resolve her conflicts into peace of mind. But I had to go on with my life and find my own peace.

I put the sale of the house into God's hands. *In his timing . . .*, I said. And I turned my thoughts to a dream-come-true trip for the summer, a writer's conference I had longed to attend for several years.

James agreed I should make the trip alone, something I had not done in over thirty years of marriage. *The conference is cheaper than a psychologist's fee,* I reasoned. And fleeting as it might have been, a glimmer of joy flitted through my head.

> *. . . keep on doing what is right and trust yourself to the God who made you, for He will never fail you.*
>
> I PETER 4:19 (TLB)

Chapter Sixteen

LETTING GO

On a bright June morning, almost one year after Dad's death, a calm voice from somewhere inside whispered, *It's time.* With an unexplainable strength, I picked up the phone and told the realtor to list Mother's house on the market.

Although I had prepared her over the previous months, she had not accepted the sale. I requested a delay in placing a For Sale sign in the yard so Mother would not become upset when I drove her to visit her sister, who lived across the street.

The realtor agreed there was no need for her to fret and stew before the actual fact of the sale, explaining months could pass before she found an interested buyer. But within two weeks she presented an offer for the house and furniture. She requested that my sister and I make a counter offer within two days.

The proposed date for closing the sale came close to the trip I had planned to New York. Diane and I decided that including the furniture with the house sale would simplify matters for both of us.

Together, we approached Mother, urging her to go with us to the house and pick out the things she wanted us to keep. She skirted our words and focused on two life-sized portraits of us as children and dozens of framed pictures of grandchildren.

"We aren't selling anything personal, Mother," I explained. "That's why we need you to help us. We don't know which bowls and platters belonged to Mam-ma Hassell. We don't know about the special meaning of some of your things.

"On the other hand, we can't keep everything," I told her. "There's a limit to the storage space in our homes. You can't use these things here in the nursing home, so we have to sell them."

PICKING OUT HEIRLOOMS

On the morning we had set aside to take an inventory of her furnishings, Mother refused to get out of bed. Diane and my daughters again begged her to go with us.

"I'm too sick," she answered, pulling the bedcovers under her chin. "You can take everything but my clock."

When Mother had moved with Dad to the nursing home, I had suggested hanging their treasured clock on one wall of their room. "No," they both said. It had continued to chime over their mantle, marking the passage of months and seasons for a house caught in a time warp.

"Do you want the clock here in your room?" I questioned.

"Yes," she nodded, her eyes half-closed. "That's all I want."

TIME STOOD STILL

Except for cobwebs in the doorways and a musty odor attacking our nostrils when we turned the key in the lock, we might have thought Mother and Dad were out for a morning stroll. Silk flowers on the table, pillows fluffed on the couch, and the weekly newspaper folded neatly on the footstool gave a "lived-in" appearance.

We set to work, cleaning out cabinets, closets, and chests. With a numb detachment, my hands sorted glasses, plates, and bowls. The walls of the house decorated with family pictures had surrounded me like a fortress during my growing-up years. The chairs and tables and beds had served my family like comfortable friends. But despite my yearning to feel something—even pain—I might as well have walked into a stranger's home.

As though I stood outside my body, I watched my sister pack china, paintings, and linens into her car. My daughters picked out quilts and photographs familiar to them since childhood. The dining room table and chairs had been an anniversary gift from me to Mother and Dad. I planned to fit them into my home.

"When we gather for family dinners, I'll set the table with Mother's best cloth and silverware," I said, wishing I could recall some good times around the massive table. "Maybe she'll feel better when we use her things. Locked up in this house, no one enjoyed them."

A CHANGE OF MIND

About mid-afternoon, Mother sent a message that she wanted to join us. "We can't bring her into this mess," I said, waving my hands at the boxes of pictures and piles of dishes in the floor. Knowing how Mother thrived on order, I had wanted her to view her home one last time with everything intact.

Diane's eyes met mine. "We asked her to come this morning," she said. "Now she'll have to wait until we get some of this straightened up."

I agreed. For the next two hours, we worked against the clock, moving and rearranging. Although cupboards and drawers were empty by the time Mother paced her steps slowly across the carpet later that afternoon, the house took on its homey appearance. She leaned heavily on her cane, her expressionless face mirroring the numbness I felt inside.

"Pick out the clothes you want," I said, leading her to a closet we had left untouched. "I'll store them at my house until the season changes."

She pulled out dresses and an old cape she had not worn for five years before she went to the nursing home. "Are you sure you'll wear that?" I asked.

"Yes, I can't get rid of my clothes," she snapped.

She looked from room to room, her eyes resting on tables and chairs. "I'll think about that tomorrow," she said.

"Mother, we told you earlier. We have to decide today about what you want to keep," I reminded her. "But she fingered jars and bottles on the bathroom vanity as though she did not hear.

"Have you done everything that you want to do?" I asked. She nodded.

"Then let's go to my house. Did you remember today is Debbie's birthday? We're having supper together."

PARTING WITH POSSESSIONS

On the drive back to the nursing home later that evening, she mumbled to herself. "I hate this place. Someday I'll walk out and start down the highway and never stop!"

The following day, I signed a counter offer. The buyers had changed their mind about the furniture, so I arranged an estate sale for the leftover items no one could squeeze into their own homes.

Mother's mood grew blacker. We argued daily over her pictures, Dad's plaques and awards from his insurance business, appliances, and a coffee table. She cried and screamed into the phone. None of my explanations reached beyond her determination to cling to her possessions.

"Those things are sacred to me," she yelled. In her flashing rage, I saw that Mother had transferred her grief for Daddy onto her home. Parting with material possessions erupted emotions that had been untapped a year before.

IN RETROSPECT

From my present perspective, I worry that I expected too much of Mother to objectively give up her material things. At the time, I was angry that she placed more stock in a house and furniture than she did in her children and grandchildren. Not that her children were unimportant to Mother. They were—but in the context she saw them.

Mother had never held interests beyond her home and her church. She had never been able to understand her children's dreams and desires when they were outside the box of what she considered a normal and appropriate role of wife and mother. She had never worked outside her home and had no understanding of interaction with people in the general public. Any person with viewpoints or traditions different from hers, she considered to be, in her words, "odd."

Although Mother demanded excellence in education from her children, she had no thirst for knowledge. She never read books nor studied subjects for the joy of learning something new. She took no interest in the financial matters of Dad's business.

Mother never juggled two things at once. If she had to attend a function, nothing else took place that week. If she entertained, all other obligations or activities ceased for two weeks. And the weather totally dominated her disposition and level of activity. A rainy day rearranged her entire schedule.

By the time we had to make decisions concerning the sale of Mother's home and furnishings, the tape player in my head described earlier by my friend was triggered into play by the aggravation, frustration, and irritation I harbored for her discontent and dependence on others. I was worn down by Mother's manipulation of my emotions.

Her unhappiness clung like a mental burr to my subconscious. No matter which direction I took, the path led back to Mother. She centered my waking thoughts. In the dark of night, bizarre dreams crept in, haunting my sleep.

Once I awoke with a start imagining that Mother had moved home against my judgment. In one scene, I passed her house and saw her sitting at the table, looking out a window. "I walked home," she called out, naming several places she had stopped along the way.

I kept Mother in the nursing home against her will when she could manage for herself, I thought with guilt racing through my dream. In the middle of the night, I second-guessed myself, afraid I had lost any ability to see both sides of the situation. *What if I have shut my mind to the fact that Mother could stay at home? Am I narrow-minded because I'm so weary? Because I don't want the responsibility of Mother at home?*

However, in the harsh daylight, I believed I had made the right decisions for her care. Coping with her complaints crowded out nagging doubts the dreams left in my mind. But daily meeting her unhappiness head on ate away at my personhood. Some days, I felt older than Mother.

> *But now the Lord who created you says, Don't be afraid, for I have ransomed you; I have called you by name; you are mine. When you go through deep waters and great trouble, I will be with you. When you go through rivers of difficulty, you will not drown! When you walk through the fire of oppression, you will not be burned up—the flames will not consume you.*
>
> ISAIAH 43:1-2 (TLB)

CHAPTER SEVENTEEN

A CALM BEFORE THE STORM

A few days before the scheduled estate sale, James and I spent a day in the city with Mother. When we picked her up at the nursing home for her routine doctor's appointment, she reclined in her chair like a limp rag doll. "I won't be back," she whispered to the staff as we wheeled her to the van.

"She believes the doctor will hospitalize her," a nurse confided when we left the home.

But as our van tires clicked off the miles, she perked up. The doctor gave a good report, and we lunched at the mall. Afterwards, we rolled her around the stores, looking at the window displays and the flowers and trees landscaping the sidewalks. As Mother's mood brightened, so did mine.

After we returned home, she phoned to ask me to keep her chiming clock. "Of course, I will if that's what you want," I answered, buoyed by what I interpreted an acceptance of the estate sale.

A FALSE READING

But the conversation took a different turn. "I'm just one little lone woman with nobody to take care of me," she began.

For the first time, I revealed my true feelings to Mother. "I have given you and Dad some of the best years of my life," I told her. "I didn't want to make the decisions I've had to make concerning your welfare, but I had no choice. And both of you have fought me every step."

"I can't help being sick," she rebutted. "I've given my life for my children and all I want is for you to love me."

"Mother, I do love you," I replied. "I've spent hours running your errands, cooking your food, paying your bills. I arranged for household help when you lived at home, talked to heads of agencies, nurses, and doctors, and waited by the phone for them to return calls. I've sat in waiting rooms through tests, office visits, and surgeries, then by your bedsides for days and weeks.

"All of this time, I could have invested in my husband, my children, my home, or my writing. But I gave it to you and Dad as a gift of my love. What more can I say or do to express how much I care?"

"I'm sorry I've taken your time," she replied in a huff.

"That's not the point. I'm not sorry. I'm glad I've been here to do these things for you. But now we have to take our present situation and go forward. I believe God plans our future at every stage of life. But it's up to us to accept His plan."

We both clicked our phone receivers into place. For the first time, I thought I had reached a level of understanding with Mother. I slept that night with a new peace of mind.

MOTHER FIGHTS BACK

Shortly before noon the next day, the nursing home phoned alerting me that Mother had fallen and cut her hand. I dashed into the nursing center as they wheeled her up the hallway, her hand bound in a bloody towel.

"She's had a stroke," I gasped behind her back to the nurse. Something about her mask-like expression and glazed eyes told me that Mother was not her normal self.

"We don't think so," the nurse replied. "Her vital signs are good. She fell in the doorway, but we can't find a place where she cut her hand."

They helped me buckle her into the front seat of my van. As I drove to the doctor's clinic, Mother mumbled incoherently, waving her bleeding hand in the air. With my left hand on the steering wheel, I tried to rewrap the cut.

In the clinic's examination room, I questioned the doctor about a stroke. He confirmed the nurse's statement. "We don't see anything to indicate one," he said. She just has a nasty cut." He put in several stitches and dismissed her back to the nursing home.

The staff helped me get her into bed. "Your mother has been very upset this week. She hasn't slept well," one nurse told me. "Your cousin came this morning before breakfast because Mrs. Ramsey called her."

My honest speech the evening before had not broken Mother's fantasy world after all. But I refused to fall into the guilt trap she had set. She needed to know how I felt and I needed to tell her. More than anything, I had wanted Mother to pick up the pieces of her life and move ahead. But if she could not, I had to for my sake as well as hers. But I knew "what ifs" would return to prick my conscience.

Mother's condition spiraled downward. Nausea came and went. She fell into a deep sleep and the doctor was alerted. He ordered her to the hospital's ER. Following a thorough examination, he arranged for a transfer to a city hospital. "Because she fell, I need some tests to determine if she struck her head," our family physician said. "She's certainly not the same woman I saw before noon today."

My cousins and aunts waited outside the emergency room. "We're going to Little Rock," I stated, stunned by the turn of events. While they waited with Mother for the ambulance, my husband and I hurried home to pack a change of clothes. We arrived at the city hospital only moments ahead of her.

ANOTHER VIGIL

For the next week, we sat by her bedside, replaying the same scenes I had experienced two years prior in a different hospital. While the doctors tested and conferred, Mother tossed in confusion. She fought the bedcovers, slapping at imaginary feathers and screaming out that something was in her bed. She insisted her furniture was in a room down the hallway, giving me a clue to her subconscious thoughts.

Could Mother have brought this episode on herself because she got so upset over the sale of the house? Did I cause this? Like weeds poking through still water, the guilty feelings I thought I had buried surfaced in a dozen questions.

"There are two chairs—a green one and a gold one. . . ." she repeated over and over. "How are we going to get them home?

"And a bedroom suite that we just bought at that little store. Did you pay for it?"

Then she would smooth the sheets on the hospital bed. "This is a thin mattress. Why did you sell my soft one?"

I explained that she was in the hospital and she did not bring any furniture. When words did not reach through her muddled mind, I tried ignoring her rambling accusations that someone had stolen her belongings.

Her turmoil boiled over in constant charges. "You don't care how bad I hurt," she said. "I just wish you'd love me."

I sat stiffly, biting my tongue to hold back angry words that I knew Mother would not understand. *Would I be sitting here in this chair for five days in a row, leaving behind everything I care about, if I didn't love you?* But I had said all that the night before this incident. I had hoped that at long last, Mother understood. But at that point, I believed she saw me only as the person to meet her needs and satisfy her emotions. She had never seen me as more than an extension of herself.

I knew I should be warm and loving, but I could not. *Is Mother really confused or is she manipulating me?* I questioned.

Her favorite nurse from the home phoned. "Nancy said she loves me two times," Mother repeated throughout the day.

Thank you, God, for someone who can say "I love you" when I can't, I prayed. *Not that I don't love Mother. I do. But love is an action, not an emotion. And right now, my emotions are numb.*

LETTING ANOTHER TAKE UP THE SLACK

Reflecting on the nurse's call on that particular day, I learned a significant lesson. I could not be all things to all people at all times, even my own mother. And it was okay for another to step in and say the loving words that I did not feel at the moment. When I refused to permit others to use their special gifts of ministry in certain situations, I robbed them of their joy.

As my caregiver's role continued over several years, I recognized that I could step in and listen to another's parent lament on worn-out subjects and remain positive. On the other hand, a fresh face and a different voice could relate to my mother's complaints without the frustration that crowded my objectivity.

LIFE AND DEATH DECISIONS

But back in the situation that demanded my attention for the moment, doctors, technicians, and nurses paraded in and out of Mother's room. They punched, poked, and peered over her body, writing notes on their shiny clipboards. One neurosurgeon ordered a vascular arteriogram to determine if she had any blockage. Mother roused enough to say, "No, I don't want it."

I hated making tough decisions for her. Decisions that could mean life and death. *What if she dies during the procedure?* I questioned myself. *Will I always remember that she said no?*

"What about the risk?" I asked the doctor.

He answered that the test and the possibility of surgery in case they found a blockage were risky. But he added that a massive stroke was a risk as well.

I signed the release, believing she was not capable of making a judgment. *Protect her*, I prayed. And I trusted God that I had made the proper decision to agree to the arteriogram.

A GOOD REPORT

The doctor reported no sign of brain damage from a fall. "Your mother had another stroke, but apparently, she's coming through it. We didn't believe she would live when you brought her in a few nights ago," he said.

I explained that I was scheduled to be away at the writer's conference for a week. "Is she stable enough for me to leave?" I questioned.

"There's nothing we can do for her that cannot be done at the nursing home," he replied. "It's now a matter of waiting to see if all the confusion lifts. Yes, I think you should go ahead with your plans."

"You are leaving on that plane on Saturday," my husband said when the doctor left. Other family members backed him up. My daughters took care of details like laundry, setting the estate sale in motion, and having someone move Mother's dining room set to my house.

DID MOTHER MASTERMIND A PLAN?

The ambulance arrived to transport Mother back to the nursing home. The attendants strapped her to the gurney while she babbled nonsense about packing up the hospital's television, two chairs, and the mattress. In my own van, I followed behind the orange-striped vehicle, praying she would be safe while I traveled a thousand miles from home.

Although the confusion continued when we placed Mother back in her familiar room, she rallied enough to tell her nurse: "I stopped that sale."

If I had been watching a movie, I might have believed that someone could have brought on a stroke to manipulate a situation. On a big screen, I would have had the advantage of insight into each character's motives and actions. Through the magic of a scripted film, I could have gotten into the heads of the players.

But it was my own mother who had admitted she made herself ill in order to get her own way. I lacked the detachment I had when viewing characters act out a scene. In the midst of complex emotions and reasoning that propelled Mother, my sister, my immediate family, and me into particular behavior, I felt overwhelmed.

I longed to hover above circumstances and look down, seeing all sides of the problem objectively. I could not accept that Mother staged a stroke. But I could believe that she worked herself into such an frenzy that she did have a stroke.

Whatever happened—or why it happened—did not alter the scheduled sale. While Mother lay in deep sleep or delusion in a hospital bed, the estate sale took place. At that juncture, there was no point in second-guessing my decision. The deed was done. I believed God had directed me to the best possible solution. On the other hand, Mother prayed to the same God and she asked for answers to contradict mine. I prayed that our personalities did not get in the way of what we interpreted as His will.

If any of you wants to know what God wants you to do, ask Him and He will gladly tell you, for He is always ready to give a bountiful supply of wisdom to all who ask Him.

James 1:5 (TLB)

Chapter Eighteen

GETTING ON WITH LIFE

"Get on with your life!" I had heard that advice from my family, friends, pastor, and therapist. I believed I was ready.

The first day at Chautauqua, New York, I tried to put behind all that had happened in the previous two weeks. Mother's state of mind and tormented face flashed in my head like scenes on a video. Eerie reminders bombarded my senses. In the 1890 hotel where we gathered for a gala dinner, I stumbled over an antique wheelchair. The old rest room smelled of urine, bringing back reminders of the odor I caught when I first opened the nursing home's front door.

At the "Symphony with Sousa" that first evening, my eyes scanned the audience from my top row seat in the amphitheater. A little brown-haired lady, moving her head exactly like Mother, sat near the front row. For a fleeting moment, the man next to her looked like Dad.

Can I possibly learn anything when my brain feels like it hangs in a twilight zone? I wondered. But seated with God's family in the Sunday morning worship service, the speaker announced his topic: "Claiming Your Stumbling Blocks." *Had I allowed Mother and Dad to become my stumbling blocks?*

I listened while the preacher read from James 1:2–3 (Phillips). *When all kinds of trials and failures crowd into your lives, don't resent them as intruders. Welcome them as friends. Realize that they come to test your faith and produce in you the quality of endurance.*

His words made me realize that Mother's depression, self-pity, and sad circumstances dominating my life left me with limited strength to minister to my husband, my children—even to her. I reaffirmed that I must commit myself to doing whatever was necessary in partnership with God to accomplish what He had planned for ". . . my future and my hope."

The speaker quoted Carl Sandburg: "Life is like an onion. You peel if off one layer at a time and sometimes you weep." Sitting in that church service among strangers, yet bonded together in a common faith in Jesus Christ, I knew I had to peel off the layers of Mother's anger, denial, and depression, and put an end to my weeping.

With a calm resolution to commit my life and its problems to God, I met the challenge of the conference classes. After a refreshing week, I returned home determined to balance my family, my writing, and my responsibilities for Mother.

I can do everything God asks me to with the help of Christ who gives me the strength and power.

PHILLIPIANS 4:13 (TLB)

Chapter Nineteen

THE CURTAIN OPENED ON A NEW SCENE

Before my plane touched the Arkansas runway, Mother set the stage for another episode. Missing her billfold from her purse, she lost control. "Someone has stolen it," she accused. The staff turned her room upside-down before spreading the search to drawers and closets of other nursing-home residents. Over the hours, the amount of money inside the leather lining grew in Mother's estimation.

The nursing home reported to my daughter. She tried to reason with her grandmother. "Don't you think Mother has your billfold?" Debbie questioned, remembering that I had dropped it in my purse when she was hospitalized the previous week.

"No," Mother insisted. "Someone stole it. They steal you blind here."

In a fit of desperation, Mother dialed the police department and reported a missing billfold with a house key inside.

By the time I reached the nursing home, the staff, weary from the problem, outlined the situation. "I have the billfold," I told them, embarrassed at Mother's outburst. "She was confused when I left, and I did not return it to her." I had told my husband that I had it, but he was picking me up at the airport when the situation escalated.

ONE STEP FORWARD, TWO STEPS BACK

The next day, Mother's emotional flare-up took its toll. She awoke lethargic and feverish. By mid-day, her temperature spiked and she was transferred to the local hospital.

"Don't let your mother control you," the psychologist has warned.

But how could I call a halt? Every time I made a step toward my own life, some crisis developed in hers. How could I strike a balance? Should I say no and walk away?

I knew the answers before I asked the questions. I could never turn away from the responsibility I felt for Mother.

A gripping ache caught my neck as though a rope wrapped around a muscle and gradually tightened. As I walked from her hospital room, I recalled reading about someone praying that Jesus would hold her grandmother's hand until she could get to her. Fighting off nausea from my exhausting trip, I fell into bed only to awaken at hourly intervals and ask God to squeeze Mother's hand and give her comfort.

HALF A SALE

In the meantime, the buyer for the house backed out on his offer. Walking through the empty rooms of her home, I wondered at the turn of events over the past few weeks.

How could I have sold my mother's possessions against her will? The question stung my conscious thoughts. *On the other hand, we were through the worst. I did what was best at the time—something that would have to be done sooner or later, I reasoned with myself. Now when the house sells, we can simply sign the papers and walk away.*

Over the next few weeks, Mother's mind muddled through the confusion of the estate sale. Her body strengthened as the fever subsided. "You sold my things when I didn't know about it," she accused.

Standing firm with my answers, I said, "We did tell you, Mother. We asked you to help us make decisions about the house and furniture, but you refused."

When the questions about furniture came, I answered with honesty. "Yes, we sold your bedroom suite."

"How much did you get?"

"Three hundred dollars."

"That's not enough. We paid $400 for it."

Each day she remembered to ask about a different chair or table. But the finality of emptying the house seemed to turn her around. As she sorted reality from the hallucinations of her stroke, I watched her half-heartedly accept life in the nursing home. For a few weeks, she let go of her self-pity and notions of being all alone.

When she showed signs of acceptance, my defenses dropped and guilt rushed in like floodwaters. I still felt comfortable with the conversation we had had before her stroke several weeks earlier. I had finally gone beyond the point of sparing feelings. Loving Mother did not alter my negative emotions. And I believed she needed to know how I honestly felt.

But Mother was a lady with rights. In my darkest moments, I lost my objectivity that her physical and mental conditions had robbed her. I fretted that I took most of them away. When the guilt of imposing my decisions on her washed over my mind, I felt as empty as the rooms of her home.

A MILESTONE

A few weeks later, we celebrated Mother's eightieth birthday. Gathered around her dining table at my home, she pointed out to guests her silverware at each place setting. I led her to the hallway to view the portraits of my sister and me. "See, Mother, we kept the things you thought were most important. Now you can enjoy them in our homes."

But her belongings in my house haunted me. Her glass canisters on my kitchen counter, the clock chiming from the dining room wall, and her rocker in front of my fireplace reminded me of Mother's consuming passion to hold onto her material possessions.

I pondered the human longing to lovingly finger a cold, lifeless object that remains after the warm, lively person is gone. Over and over in the weeks prior to the estate sale, I had said to Mother: "Those are just 'things' in your house Things you can't use. But all around you are people who love you. People are important—not *things*."

But I questioned God. *Why do material, hard, cold objects continue on and on while warm-bodied people with minds and thoughts die?*

I did not receive an answer, except for looking at my own material trappings in a different perspective. I longed for Mother to swallow the bitter pill of losing the tangible objects in her life and to involve herself with her family and friends.

One Sunday afternoon, I drove her to visit my aunts. With picture albums spread on the dining table, they laughed about things they used to do and clothes they once wore. As I watched Mother join in the fun, I remembered how often she had told me she felt shut away from her family in her nursing-home residence.

LIFE COMES FULL CIRCLE

A speaker at the New York conference had placed me eye-level with my parents' aging world when she described how children are thrust from the warm womb into a cold, bright world. As they grow, adults—sometimes looking like monsters looming over them—feed babies when they are not hungry and withhold food when they are. Authority figures tell children to go outside when they want to stay inside and to go back indoors just when they're having fun outdoors.

At the opposite end of life's spectrum, Mother experienced the same restrictions. As a nursing-home resident, someone told her when to get up and when to eat. For a woman whose major event of the day had revolved around meal preparation, she had no real choices about the food on her trays. And if a person in charge did not regulate her lifestyle, the constrictions of an aging body limited her freedom.

Despite trying to concentrate on the plus side of having an available institution to care for Mother in this stage of her life, the guilt of making my parents' decisions and placing them in a nursing home continued to weigh heavily. Each time I thought I had come to grips with the situation, it returned to fill the corners of my mind.

LOOKING UP

However, as we approached autumn, I believed we had passed a crisis. I watched Mother bond with some of the nursing-home residents and staff. High school students initiated an intergenerational program with the older people, entering the home on a regular basis for parties, programs, and visitation. She relished the sight and company of quick-moving bodies and youthful minds. One Girl Scout worked with Mother on a quilt block. But I noticed that in our conversations, she often skipped over some of the enjoyable activities.

In conferences with the activities director, she asked if Mother had told me about the recent socials she had attended. I shook my head while the director described small groups of ladies who were invited to dinner parties. In a separate room, she had set up tables with tablecloths, napkins, and centerpieces for the small group. After dinner, they participated in a special program, often remembering things of their past. The director alternated the women who came to the parties, but she had placed Mother in both groups.

"No, she doesn't tell me about the good things," I explained with a laugh. "She doesn't want me to know that anything pleasant goes on here."

WRITING DOWN MEMORIES

On a monthly basis, I began a writing class for the residents, urging them to keep their thoughts in a journal. Mother showed no interest. In fact, she balked about joining the group. But at my insistence, she agreed to attend.

I sparked their memories with selected stories about families using kerosene lamps and eating fried eggs, a slab of ham, and browned biscuits before daylight. On every occasion, Mother filled her journal with glimpses of her past that I had no idea were there.

Once she related she tried to emulate her favorite uncle's morning habit of pouring himself a cup of hot water. With the lack of coordination typical in a nine-year-old, she had accidentally poured boiling water from a kettle onto her collie dog, napping behind the wood stove. I never knew my mother had a dog.

"What was your dog's name," I asked.

"Ted," she quickly recalled. That tiny glimpse of my mother as a person with real childhood memories had been almost obscured by her obsession with the aches and pains of old age.

Although none of the residents followed through with writing down memories or thoughts in a journal, the hour we spent together each week opened up storehouses of treasured recollections. For some, I had to write their thoughts for them. A few shared verbally. Mother's writing took painstaking minutes to complete one sentence.

For a few moments, their minds took wings and their eyes twinkled as they recalled incidents from their past. I hoped they would gain new insight and appreciation of each other as they shared common experiences from days when their bodies functioned with youthful energy. Most of all, I longed for Mother to see the other residents as individuals who had led fruitful and interesting lives—and still had something to share.

But they that wait upon the Lord shall renew their strength. They shall mount up with wings like eagles; they shall run and not be weary; they shall walk and not faint.

ISAIAH 40:31 (TLB)

Chapter Twenty

ANOTHER TUG OF WAR

Mother's improved humor continued until the winter holidays. While eating Thanksgiving dinner at her table in my dining room, she took over the conversation with plans to move back into her house. "You have my couch and chair in your downstairs playroom," she said to me.

"No, Mother, I don't have any of your furniture," I replied. "Remember, we sold everything you could no longer use."

She refused to enter into any other table talk. And her dim views of nursing-home food and care surfaced again with repeated phone calls at all hours of the day and night.

MOUNTING COMPLAINTS

One early morning, our sleep was interrupted. "I've found cancer in my other breast," she exclaimed over the phone.

"Have you called the nurse?"

"Yes, I told her. I can't have surgery, but something has to be done today."

"Mother, do you know what time it is?"

"It's six o'clock," she answered.

"No, it's three in the morning. And I can't do anything about this until daylight."

Knowing we had recently received a good report from her doctor, I believed Mother's "lump" was unfounded. The next day, she centered her attention on a backache.

The calls came more frequently, often during the nighttime hours, and always in the morning before breakfast. The protests were the same.

"No one will help me. I'm dying and no one cares."

"They won't answer my call light."

"I need to see a doctor. I should be in the hospital."

Often in the evening, she would hammer nails of guilt into my heart."I won't be here in the morning," she would say, making one final tap before she slammed down the receiver.

The turnaround I thought I had seen following the estate sale reversed itself. Mother's back pain persisted until the director of nursing suggested I request a bone scan. "Breast cancer sometimes metastasizes in the spine," she warned. "Anytime someone complains of back pain, it should be checked out."

Mother's surgeon agreed and set up the scan and his routine appointment on the same day. Since I needed someone to wheel Mother's chair in and out of the buildings while I parked the van, her sister accompanied us to the city.

Following the tests and appointment, we wheeled her chair into the mall for lunch.Although I gave her the pain medication the nurse had sent with her noontime pills, Mother gave no indication of any discomfort.

After our meal, she remarked that Valentine's Day was coming up. "I'd like to get some cards for the grandchildren," she said. We rolled her up to the greeting-card counter in a drugstore and spent an hour selecting special cards. Throughout the outing, I heard no complaints of backache.

The doctor had ordered additional X rays at our local hospital. The next day, my aunt and I loaded her into the van to keep that appointment. When all the doctors conferred, they reported no cancer, but continuing degeneration typical of an eighty-year-old woman. I breathed a prayer of thanks.

NEW LIFE IN AN OLD HOUSE

About the same time, our daughter and her husband sold their house and started combing the markets for a suitable home for themselves and the new baby expected in the summer. Mother made several attempts at offering her house to them. I brushed her suggestion aside, listing the costs of putting the house in running order.

"I'll pay to have the electricity and water turned on," she said, pursuing the subject. "If it would help them out, I'd be so glad for someone in the family to live there."

Although I dismissed her proposal as impractical, I told her it was very generous of her to offer. Mother had no idea about the work and money involved in opening the house. As for her proffer to pay for turning on the utilities, she had no sense of reality about her financial resources.

I gave her plan no serious consideration until my husband and I talked one evening over dinner. Just as the voice inside my head made placing the house on the market seem right, the notion of buying my sister's ownership and renting the house to our children fell into place like clues to a mystery.

When I broke the news to Mother, she smiled in satisfaction. "I'm so happy to do this for them. You only need to vacuum and they can move in."

Once again, my spirits lifted. I made some faint reference to the necessary clean-up and repair, but it did not matter. She would not understand the cost connected to overhaul a house that had deteriorated during its three-year vacancy.

Allowing Mother to believe she's contributing to their lives might be the missing link to give her peace of mind, I thought. Latching onto any sign that she might finally be accepting her home at the nursing center, I pushed aside her life long pattern of possessiveness in relation to her house and material things.

We set to work scrubbing away the accumulation of dirt and grime at the house. Painters, window cleaners, plumbers, and electricians descended like an army.

Knowing Suzanne had resented the toll her grandmother had taken on my time and health, I questioned her about any apprehensions she might have about living in her grandparents' home.

"The good memories of growing up there are coming back," she said. "I think it may help all of us to put behind some of the guilt and resentment we've felt since Grandmother and Grandad went to the nursing home."

I nodded, hoping their furniture and their lifestyle in the house would one day erase my memories of daily prodding Mother to ride her exercise bicycle, of Dad struggling to cook and clean, and the ugly scenes when we argued over household help.

A SUBTLE SCHEME

As we put everything in working order, Mother's phone calls listing her pains and her neglect at the nursing home increased. Within a week, she suffered five falls.The doctor ordered another set of X rays to rule out a broken hip.

Although Mother had enthusiastically endorsed Suzanne and Mike moving into her house, I heard through conversations with my aunts that she laid her plans to move in with them. She described a scheme to live in one of the two bedrooms and walk two blocks to a supermarket to buy her food. The same woman who could not walk unassisted from her room to the dining hall even projected that she could help out with the new baby.

The news astounded me. Yet, I could believe her fantasies of independent living extended to such an arrangement. I had been naive to hope that Mother's agreement to someone else living in her house meant she had begun to adjust to her lifestyle at the nursing center.

I began to wonder if the constant disgruntlement linked to her continuous battle to leave the nursing home. One afternoon an aide confirmed my suspicions. "Your mother believes if she makes things bad enough here you'll take her home," she said.

And it is God who will supply all your needs from his riches in glory, because of what Jesus Christ has done for us.

PHILIPPIANS 4:19 (TLB)

Chapter Twenty-One

SEEKING MY OWN PEACE

While Mother's determination to return home loomed like a fortress, a committee convened in my head concluding, *I don't want to give anymore of myself!* A husband who first fell ill to hepatitis, then to a heart condition calling for bypass surgery, compounded my depression. And the financial concerns of our small manufacturing business struggling with a slow cash flow strained my coping skills. Other people pulled me in different directions until my personal identity was swallowed up by their needs. I felt totally unfocused.

In the eyes of my family, creating my articles and stories was a nice little pastime. But I wanted my words on paper to count for something. More and more I retreated to a secret place inside where I cherished the things that were important to me. Deep in my private thoughts, I didn't have to justify that writing was my window on the world.

In my darkest moments, I wished I had never taken any responsibility for Mother or Dad. But as soon as the thought clouded my mind, I knew that living with the guilt of not trying to take care of them would have been more disturbing than Mother's threats of impending death. At times, I wondered if I might be dead long before Mother.

WHEN YOU GET BRICKS, BUILD

One evening, newscaster David Brinkley stated: "A successful man is one who can lay a firm foundation with the bricks that others throw at him." I pondered his words, realizing that some bricks, such as my husband's illness and my mother's aging, were unintentional. Nevertheless, even inadvertent circumstances took up time and space in one's life. *But did the the pressing needs of others mean I should forsake my desire to write? Could I build something with the "bricks of life" that were heaped upon me?*

PENNIES FROM HEAVEN

A friend shed more light on my own pity party when she quoted from a speech presented to Methodist clergy. Fred Craddock, professor at Emory Candler School of Theology asked: "You know how we say, 'I give myself to you, God, to do with according to your will?'

"It's like laying a $1,000 bill out for God—except the $1,000 is me," he continued. "I give it to God all at once—all of me. But God takes the $1,000 to His bank and exchanges it for quarters! Instead of spending the $1,000 all at once, God spreads it around a quarter here and a quarter there—according to His will, which is what I committed to Him in the first place."

I felt as though God had cashed me into pennies. With every year, I, too, aged. Time passed me by with no regard for my plans and projects. *Was this God's will for me—so many duties that it took "pennies" to touch each one?*

A SEED PLANTED

One sun-splashed winter morning, my Sunday-school teacher, without knowing she spoke to my needs, touched my resentful thoughts. "Sometimes all we do is talk, talk, and talk about a problem," she said. "We know certain circumstances or persons are not going to change, so why don't we go ahead and do what we have to do and stop wasting so much energy talking about it?"

It was true. I had wasted months of time and energy reiterating Mother's problems, giving them totally to God, then slowly pulling them back into my consciousness. I knew from my counseling sessions that I had to seek peace for myself even if Mother could not come to terms with her own aging experience. Sitting in that church classroom surrounded by women who shared in my grief as well as my joys, God made it clear that I had no business obsessing on my caregiving duties or the interruption of my personal plans. He was at that moment arranging my affairs. I was where I was supposed to be; doing what I was supposed to be doing. No matter what I had programmed, He would place me where I was meant to be—if I kept my focus on Him.

After all, in the scope of His grand plan, what did it matter if the Heavenly Father spent me in dollars, quarters, or pennies?

> *. . . since future victory is sure, be strong and steady, always abounding in the Lord's work, for you know that nothing you do for the Lord is ever wasted as it would be if there were no resurrection.*
>
> I CORINTHIANS 15:58 (TLB)

Chapter Twenty-Two

MY BEST IS DIFFERENT FROM YOUR BEST

Mother typically rose to the occasion, deceiving others in both looks and actions. People who did not know us intimately could not understand why I kept her in a nursing home. They did not know her demands for health and personal care were beyond what I could cope with in any other setting.

Although I found most of her objections about nursing-home care to be unwarranted, the nagging doubts continued to creep in every time well-meaning individuals stepped on my heart and ground in guilt with statements such as, "I would never place Aunt Sophia in a nursing home! She's too alert."

Or, "Mama took care of me. Now it's my turn to take care of her."

HOW COULD I DO LESS?

One friend became so upset with a facility's incidents of neglect that she removed both her mother and her mother-in-law and cared for them in her home. My self-blame compounded when I read Bonnie Jamison's *Take Me Home*, an account of moving her invalid mother into her home for the last four years of her life. In a beautiful story, she related how her family rallied in support of giving her mother the level of care no one else could provide. Jamison's shining example made me feel as though I had abandoned my own parent.

I ached for the loneliness that I knew Mother felt. But I also recognized that many of her emotions and anxieties were basic personality traits and had no bearing on the facts of the situation. Mother lived outside the realm of reality.

She believed she would have no more sick days if she lived in her own house. Often, she stated that life would be perfect if I permitted her to return home.

In a head to heart collision I knew that, despite Bonnie Jamison's positive outcome in caring for her mother, my personality and family dynamics did not afford me the same option. I remember Mother once describing a distant cousin who devoted months and years to the total care of her mother. Even after the parent had to be placed in a nursing home, the daughter sat with her daily, bathed her frail body, changed her diapers, and fed her blended food.

Touched by her devotion, Mother related that the cousin said, "She's just my baby!"

Mother would have relished that kind of attention. I had no reservations in caring for my parent's bodily needs. In fact, I did many times. But I cringed at the idea of Mother as "my baby."

OFF-SETTING THE GUILT

Fortunately, I balanced the nagging thoughts of failure as a loving daughter with *When Love Gets Tough*, written by pastor and counselor Doug Manning. In his warm words of wisdom, Manning helped me understand that my emotions were normal. Not everyone has the same gifts. Some people have the tender feelings that convey compassion to a loved one, while others have practical natures that focus on basic needs.

For some families, taking loved ones into their homes is the best solution for long-term care. Others know their limitations and lifestyles and understand that coping with aging parents and immediate family responsibilities under one roof would be devastating for everyone concerned.

Doug Manning admits he was one of those people who boasted that his parents and his wife's parents would have a home in his house for as long as they lived. However, he observed a neighbor build a new house in order to accommodate her comatose mother who needed constant supervision. He watched her juggle a career, family obligations, and full-time home-nursing duties. Ultimately, the woman conceded she could not physically stand up to the demands of her parent's twenty-four-hour care. And Manning gradually changed his mind about the best alternative long-term living arrangements for his parents and in-laws.

CONVINCING CLAIMS

Yet, when Mother described an incident of neglect in the nursing center, I winced. I realized that her grievances were legitimate to her. And sometimes, she persuaded me with her allegations.

One morning, she related by phone that her breakfast tray had been set on a serving table in the middle of her room. From her bed, she could not reach the food or her call light.

For a moment, my temper flared. *Don't they know the doctor had ordered her to walk only with assistance? How dare they leave her food in the middle of the floor!*

I dialed the nurses' desk and ask them to check on the problem. In five minutes, the administrator returned my call. "You are right. Your mother is in bed; her tray is too far away for her to reach, and her call light is attached to her recliner.

"But," he continued after drawing a long breath, "the aide seated her in the recliner, pulled the tray in front of her, and clipped the light at her shoulder. She pushed the table away, got back into bed, and phoned you."

LINGERING DOUBTS

Knowing Mother well, I believed the answers the nurses and aides gave me matched her personality and past behavior. However, a reoccurring uneasiness that Mother could be the victim of an institutional staff fabricating incidents that contradicted hers lurked in the back of my mind. I also worried that my weariness in relating to her criticism dulled my sense of what was true and what was her manipulation.

I recognized that Mother was, for the most part, at the mercy of the people who daily tended to her needs. And like the proverbial legend about the young shepherd who fooled his townspeople with unfounded cries for help, Mother had cried "wolf'" many times. Judging her complaints proved even harder because I had experienced firsthand that many of her problems were magnified in her mind.

DROPPING IN AND CHECKING UP

Yet, when Mother accused aides of handling her roughly, I looked into matters for myself. One morning, I slipped into the nursing home as they served breakfast. I sat in the corner designated for TV viewing and observed Mother from across the room, waiting to see if the nurses and aides talked as crossly as she had said.

Although most of the staff acknowledged my presence, I believed the routine continued as normal. No one answered residents with impatience or criticism as Mother had described. I noted nurses joking with residents and some spoke to Mother. I marveled at their efficiency in getting over 100 trays on tables before fully-dressed residents.

I remembered lunch time with twenty-five of my kindergarten students. One child inevitably turned over a carton of milk; another needed help in peeling an orange. Across the table, two more could not open packages of catsup.

In what seemed like another life, I had scurried up and down the aisle between tables, patting one on the back, opening milk for another, and pointing out peas and carrots yet to be eaten. The duties of the nursing home staff were no different. Only bigger bodies cried out for help and hugs.

A RIGHT TO KNOW

However, when a nursing-home resident is dissatisfied, family members have the right to question and to observe just as the parents of my young charges had the perogative to monitor the services and administration in our school system.

Although I found most of Mother's objections about nursing home care to be unwarranted, the nagging doubts continued to color every aspect of my life

I often wished I could see my life as a movie. Then the motives and actions of others would be clear. I could discern who was right or wrong, who was telling the truth, and what the best solution would be. But life is not played out on a big screen. If it were, we would have no need to trust our Heavenly Father for wisdom in making decisions.

My approach for caring for my parents may have been different from many of my friends' plans. But with God's help, I did my best. And that's good enough.

Even when we are too weak to have any faith left, He remains faithful to us and will help us for He cannot disown us who are part of Himself, and He will always carry out His promises to us.

2 Timothy 2:13 (TLB)

Chapter Twenty-Three

A WORLD OF MOTHER'S MAKING

Mother lived in the nursing home for seven years. But it never became her home. A series of mini-strokes slowly pushed her into a clouded consciousness.

Then the dreaded day came when the staff called and reported that Mother had fallen and broken a hip. She never walked again. For the last two years of her life, she retreated to a world of her own making. Current news or happenings concerning our family or community no longer touched her comprehension.

Although she never failed to recognize me, our conversations reduced to her one-sided delusions about my dad marrying another woman, my nephews suffering tragic injuries, and an imagined neighbor boy who flooded her house with water and mowed the lawn with a vacuum cleaner.

On rare occasions, the curtain of confusion lifted long enough for a blip of clear thinking to pass through the window of her mind. On other days, she described a little newborn mouse, in her words "... no bigger than a toothpick," scurrying across the floor.

And yet another day, she imagined cats on her ceiling. "One has been dead for several days," she said, pointing to a shelf above her closet.

DIFFICULT TO DETACH WHEN IT'S MY MOTHER!

Well-meaning friends and family urged me to go along with her ramblings. As long as she talked about her sister having a baby or my dad buying a new house, I could listen. But most of the time she went into tirades about my upright dad drinking and fighting and one of her grandsons being split open from neck to toes. When she refused her meals because she thought the home served snake or rat, I could not keep up my side of the conversation.

She related bizarre details of a man, who supposedly lived across the street, killing a rat. Then she described how he dressed it for dinner. I asked her how she knew and she testily answered, "I was over at their house!"

She told me the man had lost his mind, but his pregnant wife tried to stay with him. Their little boys played in her room until 4:00 A.M. One day, she ordered me to retrieve a baby someone had left outside in the yard. She imagined she heard it "gurgle and coo."

A BABY FOR MOTHER

One of the joys of Mother's life had always been babies. I hoped my granddaughter would restore some of the affection she had lavished on babies belonging to family, friends, or even strangers.

However, Mother slipped into figments of fantasy before Jasmine was born. She rarely even spoke her name correctly, referring to the child as "Samantha." But on the day she fretted over a baby lying outdoors alone in the rain, she pulled out all stops to get my attention. "If it were Jasmine out there crying, you would go and get her!" she said.

The obsession with babies escalated. Mostly, Mother imagined the little ones were abused. She tried to wriggle from the restraint the doctor had ordered to prevent another fall and walk down the hall to rescue them. One day, she told me a particular child had its nose broken five times. She often refused to nap, proclaiming that she had to see about those babies.

In desperation, I spoke to the nursing director, asking if she thought a doll would calm Mother. She said it might—or it could make her worse.

For several weeks, I resisted shopping for a child's plaything. I could not explain my repugnance at presenting a lifeless form of a baby to my mother. When I purchased a molded newborn outfitted in a pink romper, I told Mother I had bought it for Jasmine. I asked if she would take care of it for a few days.

Immediately, she answered: "Yes, but go and get that real baby. I want it here in my room. And its shoes are in the hall. Someone kidnapped them last night."

A DOLL COMES TO LIFE

Within a few days, the doll had become the real baby to Mother. I had hoped it would divert her attention, but I was unprepared for the negative emotions I experienced when she perceived warmth in tiny plastic arms and legs. Refusing to finish her dinner, she saved food for the inanimate object she called "Katie." At times, I'd find the doll's face covered with chocolate pudding or ice cream which Mother had tried to poke down her painted mouth.

Often when I'd visit, Mother would spend all our time together trying to get the doll to stick out its tongue. She would loll out her own tongue as an example and speak "baby-talk" to the stone-cold replica of a human baby.

On one hand, I knew any comfort or pleasure the tiny imitation body stuffed with cotton could give to Mother was a blessing. Other people found her conversations with an imaginary child amusing. I might have, too, if someone else's mother had been talking to a doll.

The ultimate test with my responses came when she ranted that the neighbor boy had molested her Katie. One of the aides bustled in and out of her room on a plane above Mother's accusations about "Henry." Instead, she related that Mother fretted because one of her grandchildren had hit the other. I knew Mother was not visualizing her grandkids. By that time, she had forgotten all about them, barely paying attention to Jasmine's visits.

In all my growing up years, she had fueled an on-going feud with some of our neighbors. I realized it was still going on inside her head.

THE MORE THINGS CHANGE, THE MORE THEY STAY THE SAME

The mother I knew had slipped away. Yet, at times, her old personality surfaced even in her delusions. Often, she rambled about getting boxes to pack up her belongings for the move. Although periodically during her last two years, she believed she was at home, she never ceased to scheme about leaving the nursing home. As her life ebbed away in the final days, she begged to go home in the same whispered voice she had used when I first admitted her to the nursing center. With eyes like a terrified animal, she refused her food or medicine because she thought it was poison. I knew my mother was prepared to die. She had introduced me to her Jesus. But I sensed she was afraid. I prayed for a peace that passes all understanding.

For two weeks, I sat by Mother's bed as she slowly gave up her earthly body and went home to her Heavenly Father. I did not know the depth of Mother's spiritual understanding. But I knew she believed that Jesus Christ is the Son of God—and that is the only truth that matters.

Mother's last path on life's journey was difficult, in part because of her refusal to accept the reality of her age and illnesses. My walk with her had been rough as well, perhaps because I had tried to smooth the way on a road that each individual has to travel alone.

Even when walking through the dark valley of death, I will not be afraid, for you are close beside me, guarding, guiding all the way.

PSALM 23.4 (TLB)

CHAPTER TWENTY-FOUR

FROM WHAT WE WERE TO WHAT WE SHOULD BE

Up until Mother slipped into an imaginary world, she sprinkled every conversation with "... when I get well." She fantasized that one day she would be forty years old and living independently. I knew she regularly prayed for God to heal her. I did as well. But a quote from Charles Farr in *The Healing Choice* by Ron Lee Davis put our prayers into a fresh perspective.

Farr concluded: "Healing in Scripture does not refer to becoming as you were; it is becoming what you should be." I saw many "should be's" for Mother's life. But they were for her to work out with her Heavenly Father. I could only work on myself.

There was nothing I could do to reverse the decision I had made to place my parents in a nursing home. I could not bring my dad back to life. I could not hold back the toll of time and illnesses on Mother's body and spirit. I could not stop her complaints or give her a bright outlook on life.

SO WHAT DID I DO?

First, I acknowledged that I had done my best in caring for Mother. Despite years of feeling as though my efforts fell short of Mother's expectations, I gave myself credit for the practical and positive actions I had built into my daily routine. And I allowed myself to accept my own emotions as normal humanness.

I kept a watchful eye over her care in the nursing home. I attended the scheduled care-plan meetings with the staff. Frequently, I stopped by during lunch time to play hymns on the piano for the enjoyment of Mother and other residents.

After she lost all sense of reality, I often caught her trying to wheel her chair from the dining room as I played. She had to go and see about the baby, she said.

I continued to visit almost daily, but at different hours in order to check on care on opposite shifts. Most visits were difficult because Mother turned every conversation into a "why me?" question. But I prodded her to tell stories about her growing up. And I listened.

After Mother's physical existence turned totally inward, I made my visits shorter, typically brushing her dentures, cleaning her glasses, and listening for a few minutes to her babble about imaginary neighborhood children who hammered holes in a concrete street outside her door.

I took her special treats to eat. At my request, the dietitian printed copies of the monthly menus which I checked for meals that Mother did not particularly enjoy. On those days, I took in a lunch box of fried chicken or her favorite sandwich from a fast-food restaurant.

Up until she suffered a broken hip, I drove Mother and her sister around our scenic town. When weather and her failing health permitted, I took her to eat in restaurants and to join family gatherings.

I updated her wardrobe with bright, stylish blouses. When Mother would agree to ride in a wheelchair provided by the local discount store, I took her shopping to select her own clothes and toiletries.

As long as Mother was mobile, I took her each week to the beauty shop she had patronized for years. After she needed assistance to walk, I made appointments at the nursing-home beauty shop, checking with the beautician for special hair colors or shampoos.

I shared news of our church and the community. I took snapshots for her to view and read aloud letters from friends and family.

I included Mother in our joy in the arrival of my first grandchild—and her first great-grandchild. I took the baby for visits and encouraged her to play a unique role in forming the child's sense of family continuity.

I tried to take care of problems at the moment without judging Mother's motives. In a Bible study, my teacher noted: "If you displease God, it doesn't matter whom you please. But if you please God, then it doesn't matter whom you displease."

Her quote gave me a different perspective in my caregiving role. I did not please God when I snapped or judged Mother. I had to realize that I would never satisfy her expectations. My focus switched to pleasing Him.

In Mother's last days, I was her intermediary, requesting that no invasive medical testing be administered.

Mother suffered chronic bladder infections with fever that made her lethargic and even more disoriented. Following a painful and traumatic catherization to confirm that her symptoms were indeed due to the infection, I visited her doctor and asked him to treat her without testing. At that point if they discovered cancer or tumors, Mother was unable to undergo any surgery or extended treatment. The slightest pain terrified her. I saw no purpose in putting her through additional anguish only to determine that an antibotic should be prescribed. Our doctor agreed.

Most of all, I loved Mother—even though her manipulation and complaints strained my patience. A line from Lorraine Hansberry's play, *A Raisin in the Sun*, asks the question: *When is it time to love somebody the most? When he's done good? That ain't the time at all. It's when he's at his lowest.*

Mother experienced her lowest days living without Dad in the confines of a nursing home. I reflect that my impatience often overshadowed words or actions that expressed love. But I took comfort in Doug Manning's statement: "Love is doing what people need instead of what they want."

NO REHEARSAL FOR MY ROLE

Someone once said that living life is like playing a violin solo in public and learning to play as you go along. In the learning process, no one should expect to produce a perfect work. Parents of newborns are suddenly thrust into responsible roles with no guidebook to cover all the questions they ask or the answers they must give. By the same token, no one rehearses for parenting a parent. Each person's situation and parent is different.

Just as I made mistakes in raising my children, I made certain decisions concerning my parents that I recognize were not perfect. But in both cases, I did my best with the knowledge and resources available at the moment. I believe I did my duty in both parenting roles.

I regret that my children and my parents suffered because I lacked maturity or wisdom. But I realize that my parents made flawed decisions as well. And my children will make their own share of mistakes. Because life is a learning experience, there will always be inconsistencies, repetitions, and dead-ends. But a life committed to God's leading is an adventure, a discovery, and a training. And it is the final goal of spiritual growth that matters.

And the Lord will guide you continually . . .

ISAIAH 58:11 (LB)

RESOURCES

Carl Sandburg, quoted in *The Healing Choice*, Ron Lee Davis. Guideposts Books, 1986)

Charles Farr, *Leadership* (Spring 1985)

Ron Lee Davis, *The Healing Choice*, (Guideposts Books, 1986)

Lorraine Hansberry, *A Raisin in the Sun*, quoted in Tony Campolo, *"It's Friday, but Sunday's Comin'"* (Waco, Texas: Word Books, 1984)

The Living Bible, (Wheaton, Illinois, Tyndale House Publishers, Inc. 1971)

Doug Manning, *When Love Gets Tough*, (In-Sight Books, Inc., 1988)

Fred Craddock, Professor, Emory Candler School of Theology, quoted in *United Methodist Adult Bible Study Quarterly*, Spring 1998, writer: Karla Kincannon

Take Me Home, Bonnie Jamison, (Wheaton, Illinois, Tyndale House Publishers, Inc., 1986)

The NIV Study Bible; (Grand Rapids, Michigan, Zondervan Publishing House)